To Roman and Claire:

Two very lovely

people

Cordially

Reinhardt _____

May 18-1957

UNDERSTANDING YOUR ADOLESCENT

BERNHARDT S. GOTTLIEB, M.D.

Understanding

Your Adolescent

RINEHART & COMPANY, INC.   New York   Toronto

PUBLISHED SIMULTANEOUSLY IN CANADA BY
CLARKE, IRWIN & COMPANY, LTD., TORONTO

© 1957 BY BERNHARDT S. GOTTLIEB
LIBRARY OF CONGRESS CATALOG CARD NUMBER: 57-8069

Dedicated to

CONSTANCE, DAVID, SOLON and LUCILLE

PREFACE

THIS BOOK HAS BEEN WRITTEN to help parents understand how their sons and daughters think and behave during the period commonly called adolescence, and to help these young people understand themselves.

In some primitive cultures adolescence is either unknown or of very short duration and minor import. In our present-day Western culture, however, doubtless as a result of the complexities of modern civilization, the adolescent period is a definite entity. It has characteristics and problems that are similar, regardless of the national or ethnic group to which the adolescent belongs.

Adolescence should not be thought of as something that occurs abruptly. Physical changes of various kinds take place in every individual from the day of birth and throughout the life span. Among these changes are those that have an impact upon the adolescent. From about the age of nine to twelve years the glands of internal secretion begin to mature, and as they mature they produce a growth spurt which results in marked physical changes. It is not my intention to describe these changes. The reader who is interested in this area is referred to the many excellent books that deal primarily with the anatomy and physiology of adolescence. The present book focuses chiefly on the mental and emotional reactions of adolescence, on the psychological effects of the physical changes of this period of growth.

The reader will note that the first half of this book, Part I, describes what may be called the usual progression in psychological development. It is concerned with how the home, the school, and the community influence the young boy and girl, as well as with how the physiological changes within their own bodies affect them. The second half of the book, Part II, considers problems that arise when growth and development do not proceed normally, when some aspect of the physiological changes of adolescence, or some psychological or environmental factor has interfered with this process.

The psychoanalytic theory, or more accurately that portion of it usually referred to as the "libido theory," traces psychological development from birth onward and offers a readily comprehended explanation of adolescence. It is not, of course, the only theory that can be used for this purpose. Through years of contact with adolescents and their parents, I have found this theory useful and workable. For this reason, I have made it the supporting structure for my ideas.

I take this opportunity of expressing my gratitude to the many persons who have helped me, directly and indirectly, in writing this book. My wife, Sophie B. Gottlieb, gave me constant understanding and encouragement without which I could not have completed the task. Stella Bloch Hanau, who assisted me in preparing the text, contributed her professional skill in presenting technical material in terms that are understandable to the layman. Dr. William Schonfeld, Dr. Percy Ryberg, and Harry Urdang read the manuscript and made helpful suggestions. My four children deepened my understanding of adolescence as they passed, one by one, through this phase and entered adulthood. Finally, my patients whose experiences I have recounted have taught me much. They are, in essence, the authors of this book.

BERNHARDT S. GOTTLIEB, M.D.

New York, N.Y.
November, 1956

CONTENTS

UNDERSTANDING YOUR ADOLESCENT

This Is an Adolescent

THE TEEN-AGE BOY OR GIRL—the adolescent—is a mass of contradictions. Indeed, contradiction in mood and talk, in thoughts and action, is the key to his behavior.

When parents talk together with wry smiles or in exasperation about their teen-age children, their stories may differ in details but they are identical in their essential pattern. Adolescent boys and girls are attached to their parents and at the same time rebellious of parental authority. They are independent and helpless, idealistic and cynical, righteous and irresponsible, jolly and morose, talkative and taciturn, sensitive and callous, sociable and solitary. No wonder that they are generally hard to live with. No wonder that parents are utterly bewildered at their unpredictable behavior.

Fathers are taken aback by their young sons' vehement shouts, "I hate you," followed swiftly by a sheepish, "Oh, gosh, Dad, you know I didn't mean that." Mothers offering their daughters help in some task are irritably brushed aside with, "I can do it alone," followed speedily by, "Could you just show me, Mother? I can't seem to get it right."

The adolescent loves and hates in almost the same breath. He feels that he can do anything—conquer the world—and then he feels utterly helpless. He hero-worships his mother or father—or both of them—and then criticizes their every action. Such fluctuations of mood and shifts in action are typical of adolescence. Whether the family lives in a big city, in a small town, or in the country, whether it is wealthy or poor or

13

in between, makes no difference. The adolescent boy or girl will behave in a certain way. You and I and everyone else behaved in this way as adolescents.

The teen-age girl may stuff small towels inside her dress to give herself an "alluring figure," use heavy make-up, parade around in her mother's high-heeled shoes, smoke cigarettes in a long holder, and announce that when she is a grown woman she expects to be a *femme fatale*. But the very next day she may appear in dirty dungarees, torn sneakers, her hair uncombed. Slouching in a deep chair with feet asprawl on the window sill and hands clasped behind her head, she is lost in a phantasy world and sighs aloud, "Gee, I wish I were a boy."

Both adolescent boys and girls have conflicts about the advantages of maleness or femaleness.

Another source of difficulty is that they want to think of themselves as better than everybody else and as being able to function independently. These desires, however, lead to conflicts about relinquishing the advantages of dependency.

A father, discussing politics or war or economics with his fifteen-year-old Jack, is surprised that the lad seems incapable of sticking to the subject and proceeding in a logical orderly way.

"Do you know the population of the capital of Nevada?" Jack blurts out, quite undismayed that the question has nothing to do with the subject at hand. When his father shakes his head helplessly, Jack feels fine and quickly follows up his advantage. "Do you know the weight of a sabre-jet, the distance from the earth to Mars, the year Chrysler put out its first nongearshift model?" If the father doesn't know all the answers—as he probably doesn't—Jack struts and preens himself. He has proved his superiority. The father can understand that the lad has a great need, at his age, to feel superior. What bewilders him is that an hour later Jack comes to ask help with his homework, all thoughts of showing himself smarter than his father forgotten.

Jane gladdened her mother's heart last week by the way she took over the housework. Nothing was too much for her, and she flew into a rage when her mother suggested that her younger sister should also do her share and help with the dishes.

"She's only a kid, Mother," Jane cried. "She'll break the glasses. I can do it alone. If you'd only let me take charge of the kitchen I could manage. I'm really much quicker than you, Mother, and I don't want Beth messing in."

But this week Jane is through with housework. She refuses to lift a finger. "I did everything last week, now it's time for Beth to do something. Why do I have to do all the work around this place?" she complains. "It's not fair." Jane's mother throws up her hands. Naturally she's bewildered. She should keep ever in mind that the key to the adolescent's behavior is contradiction.

Bill dawdled around for the first two weeks of summer vacation, and finally his father suggested that he help install a system of bells for interroom communication. It will keep him occupied, the father thought, and also give him some experience. Bill is all for it, only he doesn't want to "help" his father. He will do it all himself. He will figure the whole thing out and give it all he has. He attacks the problem in a fine frenzy. He forgets about his favorite radio program, is late for meals, doesn't go out with his buddies. For days he crawls around in a tangle of wires, making diagrams, mumbling to himself, looking things up in the how-to-do-it manual. This is a big job and he can do it. Suddenly, for no reason that any adult can see, it all peters out. The project, half done, is abandoned. The balloon is deflated. The great mechanic is a small boy who won't —can't—finish the job.

Phil and Ruth—for the general pattern of adolescent behavior is the same for boys and girls—pry into the life of the adult members of the family. They turn over bureau drawers looking for "incriminating" letters, they scan old pictures hunting for family skeletons. They steam open mail over the teakettle and seal it again, and hold big sister's letters up to the light to read a stray sentence or phrase. Then they say scornfully, "I know what that big dope wrote you." They listen avidly to the home side of any phone talk between their mother and her best friend.

And then they turn righteous. "You oughtn't to discuss such things over the phone, Mother," Phil says sternly. "I heard what you said about Mr. Brown drinking too much at the club. I don't believe in drinking anyway, or in card playing. I think it's terrible the way you and Dad play bridge all the time." If Phil's mother expostulates, "How can you exaggerate that way, we play only one night a week," she is lost. There is no point in meeting Phil's criticism logically, for there is no logic in his moods, or his thoughts, or his actions.

Tomorrow, self-righteous Phil may own up to his mother that he snatched some apples from the corner fruit stand, or slipped a few toy trains in his pocket while sauntering through the five-and-ten. He may steal signs from the lamppost and tack them up in his room. To him they are trophies of his prowess, not evidence of wrongdoing.

The adolescent raids the icebox at all hours, gulping down weird combinations of food, devouring everything in sight. And then he announces a long list of things he can't bear to eat, or takes up some diet fad. He passes through a Sir Galahad period of purity in thought and deed, and then a period of fascination with smut words, pornographic pictures and running with the gang.

He is rude, overbearing, quick-tempered—and he is affectionate and kind. Roused to a frenzy by some trivial remark from his parents, he shouts, "I'm going to get out of this house. Nobody could stand living here." And he rushes away, not forgetting the dramatic slam of the front door. Soon, very soon, the phone will ring, and a tearful voice will ask if it's "okay to come home." And he is certain to exact a "no punishment" promise. There follows a period of almost overwhelming "goodness," of re-establishing himself in his parents' affection. "Can I wash the windows for you, Mother?" the runaway asks. "Can I cut the grass—hang out the wash—get your pipe, Dad," and so on.

At dinner yesterday Barbara kept up a constant chatter, giving a detailed account of everything that had happened at school. "Then I said—and she said—and what do you imagine Miss Crater did then, Mother—and then Jennie stood up and said—and then . . ."

This evening Barbara's parents expect more of the same and remind themselves sternly of the importance of being interested in their daughter's affairs. But not a word from Barbara. She is glum and silent.

"Did everything go all right at school today, dear?" her mother ventures.

"Yep."

"What's the matter, honey, is anything worrying you?"

"Nope."

If pressed to talk, there is an explosion, with invectives and blame for the parents about some upset with which they were totally unconnected.

Eric has been neatness personified for some weeks. He has bathed morning and evening, brushed his teeth after each meal, shined his shoes, ripped off his shirt at the slightest sign of dirt and jumped into a clean one, changed his socks twice a day. He has got up on time, left for school at the right moment, and come promptly to meals. It was too good to be true, his family thought; and of course it didn't last. Suddenly, day after day, he appears in the same shirt, oblivious to its grime. He can't remember to change his socks, his shoes go unshined. He is late for school, he doesn't come to the table until dinner is half over. He hasn't got time to take a bath. Why should he bathe anyway?

Bewildering? Not at all. Eric is merely conforming to the pattern of adolescence. Although he doesn't himself know what he is doing, he is actually trying to find out how important he is, he is testing his home environment to see how much he is loved. In a word, he is reassuring himself. Deep down inside he is thinking (but very likely not in words), If they like me, love me, enough, they will wait dinner for me, they won't mind my being dirty.

This, then, is the adolescent. Later in this book, I will explain *why* he acts as he does. His behavior, you will see, is not irrational but the result of experiences that are common to all people.

Contradiction, I have said, is the key to the adolescent's behavior. Why this is so is at one and the same time simple and complex. The adolescent has one foot in childhood and one in adulthood. He does not know which he prefers. The world of play and phantasy is behind him. The world of reality and responsibility lies ahead. He is faced with situations that are new and strange, that frighten and entice him. He wants to leave his familiar world and yet he is loath to go. He wants to enter the strange unexplored country that lies ahead and yet he is afraid. No wonder that he is contradictory.

And now, let us look at the situation in more detail.

PART ONE

The Adolescent's Development

CHAPTER ONE

The Formative Years—
Infancy and Childhood

WHAT HAS HAPPENED to the adolescent on his journey through infancy and childhood?

The baby has just emerged from its mother's womb. It has made its first cry and taken a deep breath. There are more cries and more deep breaths. Life has begun. For some time this little one, whether boy or girl, will travel the same road. Each of us has gone along this road, advancing from one phase of development to the next, according to a general pattern. How is it, then, that we are not all alike?

Peering through the protective glass wall of the hospital nursery, you notice that the infants differ in appearance and behavior. Some are robust and seem unperturbed; others are puny and look like worried old men. Awake or asleep, these infants do not act alike. Their cries may be loud and lusty, or weak and halting, or even low continuous whimpers. In sleep, some lie as if content and oblivious of their surroundings; others are tense and motionless; and still others constantly move their arms and legs.

It is not possible to prophesy from the appearance and actions of these babies what they will look like and be like when they grow up. Many factors, both physical and psychological, must be taken into consideration. Heredity plays a role in determining an adult's physique and personality. Far more important, however, is what happens to him as an infant and child.

Some of these infants will later be overindulged, over-sheltered and overprotected by their parents. They will grow up to be perpetually dependent or—rebelling against these forces—defiant and aggressive. Others will be rejected or neglected by their parents and will react to this lack of love by hostility against other people—that is, the world—and against themselves. Love, indifference, hate and many other factors in the environment in which these youngsters grow up will influence their behavior and their personalities. They will have different adventures in their journey through infancy and childhood, although the general pattern of their development is the same. And these adventures will have much to do with what they are like as adolescents and, later, as adults.

Let us follow any child's story from birth until about the tenth year. Baby Jim or Baby Sally—in the very early years, their story is the same—is put to his mother's breast or given a bottle. Instinctively, he sucks and this reflex action helps him get nourishment. After feeding, he falls into a deep sleep. Later, when hungry, he wakes and cries, and again he is fed and again he sleeps. When he is uncomfortable for some reason—a soiled diaper, an open safety pin, a twisted blanket, or a pain—he cries. When he is contented, he coos. His actions are automatic; he eats, sleeps, defecates and urinates. Every want, as it arises, is satisfied. Contact with his world is entirely oral—through his mouth. He lives according to his own natural rhythm, unconcerned and satisfied, with no responsibilities and no restrictions. Obviously, he is "untrained" at this time, and had best remain so.

The outstanding characteristic of Baby Jim's life when he is a few months old is that everything is done for him and that he need do nothing in return. He gets comfort and security from physical contact with whoever is caring for him. He cries, and everyone comes running—Grandmother, Aunt Mary, Big Sister, or Mother. At night Daddy joins the ranks of eager servitors, happy at the chance to get acquainted with his child. It makes no difference to Baby Jim who comes, provided they do his bidding. He is picked up, fed, cuddled, made comfortable. Through the magic device of crying, he gets what he wants, and the louder he cries, the more attention he gets. He feels important, delighted with himself and the world that turns around him.

He begins to look at his hands and feet and to grasp objects with his hands, to pick up a ball, a doll, a toy animal. His attention flits from one thing to another. His span of concentration is short. When his parents and adoring relatives laugh at something cute that he does, he imitates their laughter, rolling his eyes flirtatiously, as if gratified at pleasing his audience.

When little Jimmie is about six months old he shows attachment only to his mother or whoever is taking her place, and objects to being cared for by anyone else. Now, inevitably, Mother doesn't come with such trigger swiftness every time he cries. She may call from another room, "Just a moment, dear, Mother's coming," or she may even say, "Mother can't come just now. Be a good boy and wait."

His magical powers are dwindling. He cries louder, but no one comes. He is helpless, abandoned. His eyes search the room, he perspires, and frantically kicks and moves his arms. His thumb finds its way to his mouth; his other hand finds its way to his genitals. Tension and fear of abandonment are replaced for the moment by a feeling of comfort. Then he again bursts out crying. Even when Mother comes, lifts him up, kisses and hugs him, the whimpering continues, he is still anxious. Sometimes he is afraid to go to sleep for fear that when he wakes Mother will not be there. Sometimes his rage is so great that he refuses to eat, even when hungry. These, however, are extreme reactions. The more usual one is to cling to Mother and reassure himself by close physical contact.

When Jimmie's teeth come, he can hold fast to her, not only with his lips but with an additional tool. He bites in an effort to get ever closer to the ultimate source of comfort and safety. You can understand why Jimmie bites if you think about the inner meaning of some of the phrases we commonly use. "You darling, I'd like to take a bite out of you," people say; and "You're so pretty, I could just eat you up." The technical term for this idea is "incorporation." When we love someone, we want to be close, take them into ourselves, attach ourselves to them—"devour" them. The baby tries to do this by biting, and he bites everything that comes to hand—his mother's nipple or finger, his toys, the puppy. Don't try to keep him from biting; just give him something to get his teeth into that won't harm others or himself. If you thwart him in what is actually his attempt to cling to his mother, his love may turn to animosity and aggression, and he may use his teeth as a weapon.

Uncertainty and insecurity, and the rage that may come from these feelings, have entered little Jimmie's world. It is inevitable that this should happen, and his adjustment to the situation is part of growing up. Jimmie will be unharmed if he has been continuously loved without stint since birth. Then he can be reassured, or rather he can reassure himself that Mother has not abandoned him, that he is safe. He need not feel, as the poet has so movingly put it, "a stranger and afraid, in a world I never made."

This period in a child's life, from about eight to fifteen months, is a very important one in his personality development. He needs his mother or a good "mother substitute"—someone who takes her place in his world—not just anyone who feeds him and makes him comfortable.

I advise mothers to be with their children for a part of every day during this period when insecurity first appears, and to leave them for only a few hours at a stretch. Then even if Mother is away they will feel confident that she will soon come back. Do not go away for a week or a month, unless you leave in your place a capable and loving mother substitute. If such a person is not at hand, you run the risk of your little Jimmie developing a continuous state of anxiety, and of growing up to be an adult who is pessimistic, unsure of himself and full of mental anguish.

Have you ever watched a baby's face when you play peek-a-boo with him? Peer through your fingers when your face is covered. The baby is frightened, he thinks you have "gone away," and he breaks into a smile only when you uncover your face and "come back." When the child is willing to cover his own face, generally at about two years of age, it means that he is no longer afraid of being left alone.

The period of development that I have described is called the *Oral Phase*, since the infant makes known his wants and satisfies them through his mouth. Contact with the world is oral. The infant takes everything, and gives nothing. All of his interest is focused on himself. For this reason, the period is also called the *Narcissistic Phase*, after the youth Narcissus who loved only himself. As the Greek legend goes, Narcissus saw his own face reflected in a pool and fell in love with the beautiful smiling image. In his self-infatuation he pined away and died, and the Gods commemorated his beauty and his tragic death by the flower we call by his name. Self-love in youth and adulthood, the Greeks in their wisdom knew, leads to destruction. In infancy, however, it is normal and natural; it is the first necessary step in life's journey.

During the latter half of Jimmie's second year a start is made at establishing a routine in his daily life and at the formation of regular habits. Jimmie is awakened at a definite time, he is helped to wash his hands and face, to comb his hair and brush his teeth. He eats breakfast—usually the same foods in the same order—is helped to dress and is taken out for an airing or put in the yard to play. At a definite time, he is brought in, or called in; then he eats his lunch, takes a nap and so on. Throughout the day each event follows in its appointed way until the final ritual of goodnight kisses. Safe and protected, tucked into bed, secure in the love of those around him, he falls asleep.

Along with the setting up of this routine comes toilet training. Up to this time it has been natural for Jimmie to move his bowels and to urinate at will, and the warm urine has given him a feeling of well-being, undoubtedly like the feeling he had while in his mother's womb. Now he is taught to control these movements and to empty his bladder and bowels at a prescribed time and place. He is expected to control himself and to take some responsibility.

Jimmie's way of life is now quite different from what it was as an infant. Then he had no schedule and nothing was expected of him. He was a receiver—taking all, giving nothing. Now he must also give. Put another way, he gives up the freedom of spontaneous bowel movements, of waking and sleeping at will, of living only according to his natural rhythm, and begins to adjust to the pattern of life that society demands.

During the early days of toilet training, the child will be interested in his feces, as he looks at them in the potty or toilet bowl. It is not unusual for him to handle them, and smear them on himself and on the floor or walls of his room. He seems to enjoy the smell and the rumble and explosion of evacuation. Interest in feces and in smearing them or even tasting them is normal at this time. It is no cause for shock or alarm, however repugnant it may seem to an adult. Later, he will smear himself with food—gleefully dribbling the melting ice cream cone over his face and clothes, and if it is chocolate, so much the more fun. He will make mud pies and play with clay and enjoy finger painting. Thus he gradually substitutes socially acceptable interests for his interest in his urine and feces.

Gradually Jimmie gets to like the routine laid down for him and acquires a sense of orderliness and organization in daily living. In accepting toilet training, he gives up the pleasure of having a soiled, smeared body and in its place gets pleasure out of being clean. He becomes neat, clean, orderly, regular in his habits. He is reliable and dependable. Actually, he takes over the wishes and demands of the grownups, especially his mother. When habits and rules have become a part of him, as the saying goes, he will insist on carrying them out even when Mother is not at hand.

Woe to the inexperienced baby-sitter who thinks she will please Jimmie by a slapdash performance at suppertime. "My Mommy washes my hands before I eat," Jimmie will say earnestly, and then he will wail, "Mommy puts my milk in the *blue* mug." He cannot tolerate inconsistency and insists on the "regular" way of doing things. This trait may sometimes be a nuisance to the busy grownup, but it pays off when Jimmy says, "My Mommy wants me to hold your hand when I cross the street," and "My Mommy doesn't *let* me play with the knife."

Beneath his conformity and acceptance of regulations, however, Jimmie has some defiance and some resentment at the controls that have been put upon him. Pushing his trains around on the living room floor, to the accompaniment of his self-made chug-chugs and whistles, he doesn't come when Mother calls him for dinner. It is not so much that he refuses to be interrupted as that he cannot see why he should be interrupted. His preference is still for the spontaneity of infancy. And it is expressed in obstinacy, pushing against demands—and in delayed action.

These tactics are clearly shown in some of the ups and downs of toilet training. Sometimes Jimmie holds back instead of giving up his bowel contents each day. He refuses to have a movement today, so that he can "spontaneously" empty his rectum tomorrow. When Jimmie makes a fuss about getting ready for bed or taking a bath, when he refuses to dress himself in the morning he is using delayed action techniques in his battle against authority.

On the whole, however, if the mother is calm and patient, kind and tender, but firm, Jimmie accepts training and routine. He likes the orderly life that is set up for him, and enjoys being a "good" clean little boy.

The period during which these events take place is called the *Anal Phase*. In the carefree Oral Phase, you will recall, the child's interest was focused on his mouth. With the acceptance of some responsibilities in this second phase of development, his interest is on the anal region. If Jimmie's mother has carried through his training with love and the least possible amount of sternness, if she has been successful in establishing mutual understanding, Jimmie will have a feeling of freedom even though he acknowledges discipline. He will have a sense of security and happiness, and he will be an outgoing and friendly child.

Starting at the age of about four, or perhaps a bit earlier, we can no longer tell any child's story—boy or girl—in terms of what happens to Jimmie. From this time on, girls and boys meet with somewhat different adventures.

Both Jimmie and the little girl of four or thereabouts—let us call her Sally—become interested in their genitals and those of their playmates, and notice the anatomical differences between boys and girls. Their reactions, as might be expected, are not alike, however; neither are their attitudes toward their mother and father.

Jimmie has already been taught how to stand up at the toilet and hold his penis to urinate. Now he happens to see his father undressed, and is shocked and upset at how large Daddy's penis is compared to his own. He has already noticed that his penis gets larger when he touches it, and so he gets the idea that he can perhaps make it as big as Daddy's by playing with it. This is an ambitious program, something forbidden, that must be done in secret. His hand has perhaps been removed gently— or slapped—when he was caught playing with his penis. Perhaps he has been sternly told never, never to touch it except when he urinates. He must try to make his penis large without being discovered. What will happen if he is caught handling his genitals? He feels anxious and guilty. He envies Daddy and hates him, and he hates Mother for being friendly with Daddy and so fond of him.

Lying awake in bed at night, Jimmie hears his parents talking happily together in the living room. In the morning he finds them together in bed. He wants to sleep with Mother, but he is not allowed to do so. At every turn, his father seems to thwart him and stand between him and Mother, claiming from her the affection and attention that he wants for himself. Not only in his secret thoughts about his father's large penis, but in actuality as he looks up at this tall man, Daddy seems to be an all-powerful giant with whom he is unable to compete.

So Jimmie turns to competing with other boys, people nearer his own size. You may have seen a group of five-year-old boys line up and urinate in unison, each one trying to beat his companions in throwing the stream in a wide arc. Jimmie looks at the other boys' genitals, with reactions of satisfaction or disappointment according to whether they are smaller or larger than his own. Experimentally, he touches another boy's penis to see if it gets bigger. He is envious and frustrated. Jimmie and his comrades—for they are all in the same boat—release their feelings in anger and fist fights.

And what of Sally during this period? As I have pointed out, her reactions are not the same as Jimmie's. When she becomes aware of her genitals and of the anatomical differences between herself and boys, she finds that she has no appendage such as Jimmie has. She is bewildered. Will it grow later, when she is a big girl? Has it been taken away as a punishment because she disobeyed Mother and played with herself? Even if Sally has seen her mother in the nude, she does not make any connection in her mind between her mother's body and her own, and has probably not even noticed that mother has no penis. At this age, Sally is not able to arrive at any general concepts about "all women and girls" as an adult naturally would. She is concerned only with her own lack of a penis. Perhaps, Sally thinks, Mother has destroyed her penis. She is angry at Mother and doesn't love her any more. Her hostility is openly expressed in refusing to obey Mother's orders and even destroying some of mother's treasured belongings. But these acts of rebellion only increase her distress, for she fears that Mother, who is so much bigger and more capable, will retaliate.

She turns to Daddy for comfort, only to meet with frustration. He pays more attention to Mother than to her. Like Jimmie, Sally hears her parents talking happily together while she lies awake alone in her room. Like him, she finds Daddy and Mother together in bed. In Sally's case, however, it is Daddy she wants to sleep with, and Mother whom she resents as coming between them.

And now it generally happens that a disturbing complication is added to the situation for both Jimmie and Sally—the arrival of a baby brother or sister.

Although the youngsters have been prepared for this event according to the modern approved custom, they have not realized the change that it will make in their lives. Mother is busy with the baby. Grandparents, aunts and uncles, cousins and friends gather round to admire the new little prince or princess. Jimmie and Sally feel left out. Despite their hostility to Mother, they achingly want her attention and love as in the past, and now they must share it with this interloper. Hurt, bewildered and jealous of the baby, it seems to them that Mother has no concern for them at all.

Mother holds the baby, nursing it or giving it a bottle. Jimmie, too, wants her to hold him and feed him. Mother changes the baby's soiled, wet diaper. He, too, wants this attention. In a futile attempt to gain his ends, Jimmie may revert to bygone infantile habits. He may insist on drinking from a bottle instead of a cup. He may wet and soil his pants. But Mother quite possibly doesn't wash him and put fresh pants on him, cooing and clucking as she does with the baby. She may only scold him. "Shame on you," she may say, "a big boy like you acting like a baby." Sally, too, may revert to infant ways in an attempt to get her mother's attention. The very worst thing a mother can do in such a situation is to shame a child by putting him into diapers and rubber pants. She should try not to show her disapproval by word, deed or expression. If she understands why the older youngster behaves in this "odd" way, she will be able to tolerate it.

Jimmie is confused, unhappy and resentful. He cannot compete with the baby any more than he could compete with Daddy. He tries to get even. Left alone with the baby, he hits it and it cries. Mother rushes in before any serious damage is done. She scolds him and he feels guilty. This sense of guilt is increased if the baby is a boy and has been circumcised. Jimmie notices, while watching Mother diaper the baby, that there is a small reddish-brown scab at the head of its penis. Could this be some punishment for having masturbated? Could the same thing happen to him? Jimmie is frightened and cowed, and resolves to be "good." If the baby is a girl and he sees that she has no penis, he is even more frightened. Sally, disturbed like Jimmie by the loss of her mother's interest and attention when the new baby comes, also reacts to the presence or absence of a penis in the infant.

This period in a child's development is called the *Phallic Phase*, from the Greek word *phallos*, meaning the male generative organ. In ancient Greek religious rites, the *phallos* was the symbol of fertility. During this period, concern with anal activities diminishes and attention is focused on the genitals. Parental understanding, especially if a baby is born while the older boy or girl is in the Phallic Phase, can do much to lessen the child's feelings of inadequacy and guilt. Above all, keep in mind that masturbation is normal and natural, and that it should not be forbidden or punished. It is not masturbation in itself that is harmful, but the guilt feelings that arise because of parental attitudes about it.

Further changes take place when Jimmie and Sally are about five or six years old.

Jimmie has been frightened into abandoning his secret plan of making his penis as big as Daddy's by masturbating, and has stumbled on a better way of gaining his ends—through phantasy. In his play activities he carries a cane or stick, a sword or a toy gun. His symbolic penis is longer than those of the other boys and he keeps it close at hand, awake and asleep. His magic weapon protects him from all harm. Now he can compete with other boys. He can even compete with Daddy, he feels, and his anxiety, jealousy and guilt diminish; his self-confidence is regained.

He will be so like Daddy that even Mother will notice it and give him the same attention and love. And so he mimics his father, acting out the role of the man of the household. Returning from school, he kisses mother, puts on Daddy's slippers and pretends to puff on Daddy's pipe. "Hello dear," he says, with a good imitation of a tired man's yawn. "Had an awfully hard day at the office. Hope you've got a good supper ready." And significantly, he will say to his mother earnestly, "If Daddy dies, I'll marry you and take care of you."

Sally, as might be expected, tries to play the mother's role. Her interest in Daddy increases, and—as she works it out—if she is like mother, then Daddy will pay attention to her. She puts on mother's dress, high-heeled shoes and furpiece, slings mother's purse over her arm or shoulder and dabs mother's lipstick and powder on her face. As a final fillip, she douses herself with mother's perfume. Still Daddy gives Mother the preference, and Sally becomes more and more jealous.

Aping Mother, Sally plays house. She bathes and nurses her dolls, and cooks complicated imaginary dinners on her toy stove, busily preparing for her "husband's" homecoming at the end of the day. Suddenly she is rudely shaken out of her phantasy when Mother calls, "Sally dear, stop playing now and come take your bath." Her dream world collapses. She wasn't "playing," she was taking care of her home and children, and now Mother has made her just a little girl. She won't stop. She won't do anything Mother says. She hates Mother.

But if Mother discovers how I feel, Sally figures, she'll punish me. Aggression, bewilderment and guilt—and yet a desire for Mother's love—are all mingled and confused in little Sally's mind.

The mother is also confused. What has happened to Sally, who was such a sweet good little girl and is now so stubborn and rebellious? The mother should try to understand the basis of Sally's behavior, and keep in mind that it is a temporary phase. Then she will be able to meet her daughter's aggression with devotion, kindness and firmness, and above all without tit-for-tat aggression and emotionalism. Sally will soon recognize that she has nothing to fear from her mother, that she need not feel hostile toward her. Mother is willing to *share* Daddy, she realizes. So she begins to be a little companion to her mother, to help care for the baby brother or sister instead of resenting the infant. Some day she will have a baby of her own—with Daddy.

This period of development is called the *Oedipal Phase*. It takes its name from Oedipus, who, according to the Greek legend, unwittingly killed his father and married his mother. The Fates had prophesied at his birth that this would happen and it came to pass despite all human efforts to prevent it. The idea that men fulfill destinies laid out for them by Fate is foreign to our way of thinking, for we believe that we can make of our lives what we will. Yet the story has fascinated poets and playwrights from the days of the great Greek dramatists five hundred years before the Christian era down to the present time. Doubtless the reason is that deep in everyone, largely unrecognized and certainly not acted upon, is this love and desire for the parent of the opposite sex.

Such considerations, however, take us far afield from our story of Jimmie and Sally. Enough to point out that in the Oedipal Phase the little boy attempts to win for himself the love and attention that his mother gives to his father, and the little girl seeks to gain her father's love and attention. These feelings are not, of course, definite and clear-cut, with exclusive focus on one parent. There is, however, a well-defined pattern of Jimmie's seeking Mother's love and Sally's seeking Daddy's.

And now, generally at about the sixth or seventh year, comes the *Latency Period*, during which the earlier interest in the genitals and in anatomical sexual differences between boys and girls diminishes and interest in the outside world increases. The sexual drive for love becomes dormant. As the term "latent" implies, this drive is not lost, but only concealed. It will rise to the surface again in adolescence.

Jimmie and Sally have an insatiable thirst for information about everything in the whole wide world, in the heavens, and beneath the earth. The limits of their personal life now extend beyond their parents and the immediate family circle to take in other adults. Curiosity is perhaps the outstanding characteristic of the Latency Period. Another characteristic is the desire to own things. The youngsters become avid collectors, and it makes little difference what they collect. Butterflies, stamps, or ferns; bottletops, empty match covers, buttons, pieces of string, silver foil—all are equally exciting. They want to know why the leaves are green, why the birds sing, why the car backfires, how the radio works, and so on and so on. They must see everything, learn everything, understand everything. The world is full of things to see and do, to have and to make.

One thing that Jimmie and Sally and their playmates are curious about is the origin of babies. They have long since rejected the idea that the baby is bought at the store or brought by the stork, and they know this much—that it grows in the mother's belly. How it got there is the puzzle. Some think it begins when certain foods are eaten, or when the parents kiss each other. Another puzzling thing is how the baby is actually born. Is it vomited out through the mother's mouth? Does it come through the anus? Perhaps the belly button opens up, or the stomach wall is cut to make a passage. Children exchange views on these matters. Despite the modern attitude of free and open discussion between parents and children, the youngsters generally speculate about the subject and talk about it in secret.

Babies are not the only thing that they talk about. Jimmie, in an effort to increase his importance among his comrades, may spin out some fantastic tale which he and all the rest know need not be accepted as true. "My uncle just came back from Africa," he may say. "He brought me a baby elephant and a tiger." No one asks to *see* the tiger! And Sally may recount some bit of family history that was not designed to be heard by the big ears of the little pitcher, and certainly not by the ears of all the other little pitchers.

All these interchanges of secrets—absurd as they may seem to the adult—serve a good purpose. They are a necessary part of a child's development, in that they help him establish relationships with other children and give him the experience of close contacts through common interests and mutual loyalty.

Jimmie and Sally actually have similar interests during the Latency Period, but this is sometimes not apparent because adults have preconceived notions of special things that boys and girls are interested in and like to do. Arbitrary notions about different occupations for boys and girls are being abandoned, however, and there is a general tendency today for both girls and boys to be taught cooking, sewing, carpentry and so on.

School looms importantly in Jimmie's and Sally's world during the Latency Period. Some children have been to nursery school and kindergarten before starting the more serious business of the first grade, and have already adjusted—or possibly not adjusted—to close contact with a woman other than the mother, namely their teacher. I shall discuss this adjustment in greater detail in a later chapter.

All that happens at school is, at first, recounted daily at home, with the child acting out the events to the accompaniment of verbatim reports—he said, and I said, and then he said, and then she said. Gradually, the child becomes more selective and impersonates only the more important characters—the teacher, the principal, the best friend. He also impersonates movie stars and heroes in the sports world. Fact and phantasy are mingled in his accounts of actual happenings and make-believe situations.

Today, Jimmie is firing an imaginary tommy gun, and the house resounds with his "ack-ack-ack" as he sprays the enemy with its deadly fire. Tomorrow he is a knight, jousting with a broomstick lance. Sally is warbling like Mary Martin—she *is* Mary Martin, bowing and smiling as the audience claps. She is Elizabeth, receiving her crown, a beggar maid beloved by a prince. Everything is grist to the youngsters' mill and everything is real.

Identifying himself with the heroes of the radio, TV and movies, and with persons in the public eye, the child looks up to those in authority at home and at school. There is a minimum of protest and irritation, and the precepts of the parents, whatever they may be, are accepted and followed.

This is the period in which children first experience the pleasure of banding together in organized groups, such as Cub Scouts and Brownies, the forerunners of Boy and Girl Scouts. Such groups help children develop attitudes of honesty, reliability, co-operation and identification with authority. The child who belongs to a club accepts his companions and is accepted by them. He learns at firsthand some of the principles of democracy and of interpersonal relationships.

Jimmie (or Sally) may by temperament be a leader. If so, he will develop skills in his club activities that will stand him in good stead in later life. He may, however, be a follower, and his parents should be happy if he learns to be a good one. There is need in the world for both leaders and followers. Ambitious parents often do their children harm by forcing them to take positions in their group life for which they are not temperamentally suited.

Not all children are joiners. The reasons why they avoid group activities are many and complex. Perhaps a lad has attempted to be a leader and has failed. He may then turn to isolation as a solution, playing alone, acting out the role of successful leader in phantasy. Another lad may feel physically or mentally inadequate, and may avoid group activities in order not to be forced to compete with his peers. Still another may want to stay close to his mother, or he may be uncontrollably pugnacious and become a solitary to avoid trouble. Whatever the reason, the child who consistently isolates himself from all group activities should not be left to go his way. He should receive special and immediate attention in an effort to get at the cause of his behavior, for it may be a sign of serious maladjustment.

All groups, unfortunately, do not have constructive aims. Some of them try to protest against authority by stealing, fighting, and destroying property, by acting tough and talking tough. In such a group or gang, the youngsters will gleefully use dirty words and talk smut, feeling that this makes them grownup. Such language cannot be controlled by threats and punishment; such action only makes the words seem more important to the child. Far better to let them pass unnoticed. Then they will lose their significance and be quickly forgotten. Far more important than the use of dirty words are the pugnacious and destructive things that such a gang may do. As I have said

above, normally the child in the latency period accepts authority. When he does not, something is amiss. Later in this book
I will try to explain what sets him on the wrong path.

During this period Jimmie and Sally think a good deal
about God and about death. They ask questions and want to
know—specifically—what Mother and Daddy believe. Perhaps
the death of a beloved grandmother or uncle or dog gives them
for the first time the idea that their parents will some day die.
Up to this time, the parents have been immortal, so to say, and
the thought that they will not always be at hand has never
arisen. Feeling the need for someone always close, sensing that
this mysterious thing adults call death may take away the
parental support they have always known, the children shift
their dependence to God. Thus they maintain their feeling of
continuous and ever-present security. The child at this age
believes, as he may never again in life believe, "His eye is on
the sparrow and I know He comforts me."

Jimmie and Sally are now about ten years old. They have
passed through the oral or narcissistic phase of infancy, the
anal phase of habit formation, the phallic phase of interest in
the genitals, the Oedipal phase of love for the parent of the
opposite sex, and the latency period when these drives are
dormant and interest is focused on the outside world.

This account of the formative years of infancy and childhood is much simplified and all too brief to do full justice to
the complexities of the subject. I am well aware—and I beg the
reader to be aware—that much has been left unsaid. My purpose in giving this brief summary is to help you understand
your children and also yourself. You will be better able to do
this if you keep in mind the main characteristics of each phase,
as I have described them.

The actions of the child in each phase are normal for that

particular time in his development. Generally, most of the characteristics of each phase are sloughed off as the child grows older and becomes immersed in the following phase. Only small traces carry over and are retained in the adolescent and in the adult. These are the factors that determine a person's basic personality.

In other words, the growing child normally retains something—but not too much—from each phase of his development through infancy and childhood. Sometimes, for one or another reason—generally the parents' attitude—too many of the characteristics of some one phase are retained. This is what you are saying when you shrug off the pranks of forty-year-old Bill Smith with the remark, "He's an overgrown boy." Only, at forty, it isn't normal for him to act like a boy; if all had gone well, he would act like an adult. You may try to excuse selfish and irresponsible Mrs. Jones, mother of three children, by saying, "Oh well, what can you expect; she's just a child." What you mean is that she has kept too many of the characteristics of the oral phase of her life. Bill Smith and Mrs. Jones were caught, as it were, at some stage of their development. The technical term is "fixated." They kept to too great a degree the characteristics that were normal and natural for a phase of childhood but that should have been left behind as they advanced toward adulthood.

Let us take some examples from childhood itself. If a child has been disappointed in his drive to "obtain" during the later part of the oral phase, he may grow up to be anxious, pessimistic and hostile. Instead of his interests being diverted from the mouth to the anal region, as they are in normal development, they are fixated at the oral area. As if he has never had his wants sufficiently satisfied, he still wants to devour, to bite and make people suffer—or to suffer himself. A child who has perhaps been overtrained during the anal phase, the time of habit formation, may retain too many of the characteristics of this period. He may later on be overmeticulous, oversystematic, and overorderly, too concerned with small unimportant details, too prone to magnify insignificant things and events out of all proportion to their relative value.

All this may sound pessimistic. The world must be full of misfits, you may say. Actually this is not so. A healthy child, reared by understanding parents who have themselves attained to a good level of maturity, keeps the useful components of the phases through which he passes on his journey toward adolescence, with a minimum of fixation and a maximum of flexibility and integration. If he has been loved and feels emotionally secure, he will have the two elements essential for a happy useful life.

And now, let us see what Jimmie and Sally are like as they leave childhood behind and enter adolescence.

CHAPTER TWO

The Stuff That Boys—and Men—Are Made Of *Early Adolescence*

IF YOU WANT TO UNDERSTAND your adolescent son, try to keep two things in mind.

First and foremost, he is in a state of indecision, although in all likelihood he is not himself aware of it. Should he remain a child, with the comfortable advantages of childhood dependency? Or should he be—or at least try to be—an adult and accept the difficulties and the heady challenge of that role? Second, as I have explained in the previous chapter, he shows traces of all the phases he has passed through during infancy and childhood, and sometimes he is fixated at one or another level of his past development. When this happens, the characteristics of that level dominate him to the near exclusion, or at least the overshadowing, of other traits.

As a result of all these complex reactions, Jimmie is full of contradictions and unpredictable actions and moods. He veers sharply first in one direction and then in another. The technical term that is used to describe this two-sidedness is "ambivalence." The word comes from the Latin *ambo*, meaning *both*, and *valere*, meaning *to be strong, to be worth*. Thus, ambivalence means giving weight, strength, worth, value to two things, two emotions, two ideas, or two lines of action at the same time. It means loving and hating, accepting and rejecting, being sociable and unsociable, feeling and doing these apparently opposite things almost simultaneously.

42

Ambivalence is the key to the mysterious ways of the adolescent boy. Let us look at him more closely.

When, you may ask, does adolescence begin? There is no fixed age, just as there is no fixed age at which all children begin to talk or to walk, or at which they pass through the various phases described in the previous chapter. For some boys, adolescence begins as early as the ninth year, for others at twelve or thirteen, or even as late as fifteen. We must not confuse adolescence with puberty. The latter refers directly to the physical changes that occur during the period when certain secretions from various glands induce a growth spurt and cause the body to lose the characteristics of childhood and take on the characteristics of adulthood. Most of these changes take place without the individual's being aware of them, and hence they go unnoticed for perhaps as long as a year. This is the period of puberty or preadolescence. When the boy recognizes the various changes that are taking place in his body, we can say that adolescence has begun. The first physical sign of adolescence is growth of hair on the face and around the genitals; the first psychological sign is the boy's interest in these bodily changes.

One morning, when you call to Jimmie to hurry and come get his breakfast, there is no answering shout. You open his bedroom door after a perfunctory knock, all set to pull the covers off and rout out the sleepyhead. But he's not in bed. He's standing in front of the mirror, squinting at himself with absorbed interest and concentration. Cheeks taut, lips pursed, he is running his fingers over his chin, feeling with glee the first indications of the change from the smooth face of childhood to the bearded face of manhood.

Make no mistake. Jimmie's adolescence has begun. Whether this period will be stormy for him—and for his family—depends on many complex factors. It depends on how he was handled as an infant and child, how well or ill he was guided in each phase of his development, and above all on the support, patience and understanding given to him during this last part of his journey into the adult world.

Jimmie is peering into the future. The curiosity that characterized him in the Latency Period is intensified. If he is a reader, he is obsessed by the idea of the thousands upon thousands of books in the world—he wants to read them all. If he likes mechanical things, as almost all boys do today, he wants to know what makes them work. He will take clocks and radios apart and dismantle an automobile engine if he has the chance. The bulldozer at work on a new road, the giant crane swinging steel girders into place for a skyscraper command his wrapt attention. (Incidentally, the sidewalk superintendents to be seen at any building site in a large city are not all adolescent boys. Most of them are men who still retain this engaging curiosity from earlier years.) Trees, snakes, fish, guns, baseball, mountain climbing, astronomy, chess, carpentry, a fingernail clipping under the microscope, hiking, sailing—it is not possible to list all the subjects that interest an adolescent boy.

Enough to say that his curiosity—his need to know—ranges far and wide and is insatiable. Specifically, he wants to know how animals and people began, how babies are made, and how a boy grows up to be a man. All his activities and questing are in final analysis attempts to understand these mysteries.

The appearance of hair on his face makes Jimmie proud. It is a sign of manhood. Yet it makes him self-conscious (remember that he is ambivalent) and he is shy and uncomfortable if anyone refers to it. The change in his voice also pleases and upsets him. He tries to pitch his voice low and is embarrassed when a sentence begun in manly bass tones ends up in a childish treble. Easier to keep quiet, he may feel, and not talk at all. A trip to the store on a simple errand may seem a major undertaking, to be carried out with trepidation. He may have a sinking feeling in the pit of his stomach as he buys a loaf of bread for his mother. Then again, he may be incisive and brusque, greatly fancying himself for the efficiency with which he carries through this assignment.

Jimmie and his friends discuss the changes that are taking place in their bodies. They examine each other, note the amount of hair they have and boast about having to shave. They discuss many things that puzzle them and that they are unwilling to discuss with their parents—nocturnal emissions, masturbation and their thoughts and phantasies about sex. By this time they probably know about reproduction and intercourse, and very likely they are aware of the fact that their parents "indulge sexually." But even if they have been reared in the modern way where there is no hint of furtiveness about sexual matters, they sense that this aspect of their parents' lives is not talked about openly, that "something" goes on in the parents' bedroom that they are not supposed to know about. They are ashamed, and they gain a measure of reassurance by discussing the matter with their comrades in strict secrecy.

Much of their talk centers around pornographic pictures that fall into their hands in school and on the streets. To see sex details in pictures and in print, "proves" that the sex act is not phantasy but actually takes place and is "real." To share this knowledge with others lessens each lad's sense of fear, anxiety and guilt about this strange and mysterious event.

You may be resentful that your son talks to other boys about such important matters instead of to his parents, or at least to his father. Any man who takes the trouble to recall his own youth will understand that this is natural.

In addition to his close, natural relationship with his

friends, Jimmie wants to be alone. He wants privacy to dream and to indulge in sex phantasies. If he has a room of his own —and every effort should be made to give him one—he will keep the door closed and hang out a sign, *Do Not Disturb*, or *Genius at Work*. Much of his "work" is probably keeping a diary, to which he "tells" everything. The diary does not criticize or blame. During the day he had to keep still while he was scolded by Mother or Dad or his chemistry teacher. Now he can answer back, justify himself, and do in phantasy what he did not do in actuality. He can recast the events of the day, in which he perhaps showed up badly, and make himself a hero.

The adolescent's diary is in a sense a substitute mother. When he was a small boy, his mother urged him to tell her "everything," and this he did—omitting some small naughtinesses. The adolescent still needs a sympathetic and ever-ready listener. But too many things would now have to be left unsaid. Instead of the minor offenses of childhood that could so easily be left out of his accounts of the day's doings, he now has thoughts and acts that could not possibly be told to another human being. The diary is the perfect solution.

Jimmie often imitates the style of prominent authors, living and dead, as he writes down his secret thoughts. In his phantasy, he may actually *be* some favorite author, suffering his woes, enjoying his triumphs. Jimmie's diary is his treasure, carefully put away or locked up for safety. Woe to any member of the family who pries into it.

Safe in his own room—his castle, where a bolt or a turn of the key raises the drawbridge and protects him from intruders—Jimmie also has ample opportunity to masturbate. You will recall that I spoke in the previous chapter about how infants instinctively seek comfort through masturbation, and how small Jimmie in his Phallic Phase masturbated in an effort to make his penis as big as Daddy's. Masturbation, then, is in itself not a new experience in adolescence, but it differs profoundly from the same action in infancy and childhood. Then it was a mechanical process; in adolescence it is accompanied by phantasies of sexual contact with a woman and by imaginings of a sex and love relation for which the boy is not yet ready. Confronted with an actual female sex partner, he would be frightened and incapable of enjoying intercourse. Sufficient for the present to have phantasies. The earliest ones may be about a variety of women, and they invariably include his mother. Many boys in their earliest phantasies have as a vague image only the mother, the first love object. Later, the boy thinks more concretely of popular actresses and pin-up girls, of the provocative females in the bra and girdle ads, and the exciting sirens whose pictures tell the world of beautiful stockings and alluring nightgowns.

Much harm has been done by parents through trying to make their sons promise to abstain from masturbation. No matter what the parents say, they will continue to masturbate, and they will have a great sense of guilt and shame about it. (They will have some guilt anyway, even if the act has not been explicitly forbidden.) If you have followed me thus far, you will understand my saying that it is entirely natural for your adolescent son to masturbate. Do not make an issue of it. You should, however—and I speak here to the father, not the mother—have the sort of relationship with your boy that makes it possible to discuss sex matters with him, including masturbation. And you should give him information about nocturnal emissions *before* he reaches adolescence and has this experience. The father or whoever is taking the father's place, not the mother, should explain emissions and their physiological significance.

A lad who has not been given this information may be

very much disturbed and upset when he first has an emission. The sticky semen with its musty odor, clinging to his pajamas and the sheet, frightens him. What has soiled the sheet? He knows it isn't urine. It must be hidden from Mother; it must be hidden from everyone and kept secret. His usual high spirits change to sullenness and perhaps complete silence. Questioning by his bewildered parents only calls forth denial of any difficulties. Thus he is emotionally driven away from his parents just when he so greatly needs their support.

If the phenomenon of nocturnal emissions has been explained, and the boy knows what to expect, he eagerly awaits his first experience. When it comes, he is curious and perhaps surprised, but not frightened. He may, in fact, be exhilarated at this indication of approaching manhood. He accepts emissions as normal and natural, as something that happens to all boys in the course of their physiological development from boys to men.

If Jimmie has had this preliminary information from his father, and mutual understanding has been established, it will be easier for him and his father to talk about many of the things that puzzle and bother him in adolescence. By this time Jimmy probably knows that masturbation does not produce mental illness, venereal disease, sterility or impotence. Nevertheless, he has a vague sense of guilt and anxiety and needs reassurance. His first sex phantasies, often so buried that he is not actually concious of them, have centered around his mother. This, of course, cannot be "confessed" to his father. So, the boy at one and the same time seeks to be close to his father and yet rebuffs the father's attempts at closeness. He backs and fills.

The father also has contradictory feelings. Many men admit that they feel uncomfortable when they try to talk with their adolescent sons about sexual matters. This reaction does not come from prudishness. It has a more complex cause.

Every adult has experienced the pleasurable or frightening excitement that comes from talking about sexual matters, whether with someone of the same or the opposite sex. It is as though the two persons, by some strange alchemy, are experiencing a kind of disembodied sexual relationship. It may seem strange, but if you think it over I believe you will see that in the father-son setup, the father veers away from sex discussions with his son because he is unconsciously recoiling from this kind of disembodied relationship. At the same time he wants to be close to his son and discuss things with him helpfully and frankly.

If both father and son can disentangle their ambivalent reactions, if they can base their relationship on shared interests and activities, and on mutual love and respect, they can establish a relationship that will be fruitful for both of them. When such a relationship is achieved, the boy—grown into manhood—will be able to have wholesome friendships with other men. When it is not achieved, his adult contacts with men are likely to be carry-overs of the confused father-son situation of his adolescence.

All too often an adolescent boy's father is not the kind of person he can admire or try to pattern himself on. And in some homes the parents have been separated by divorce or the father is dead. The lad will then try to make a father-son relationship with some other man—an understanding teacher, a club leader, or camp counselor. This often works out in a very satisfactory way. If no such person is at hand, he will focus on some national figure, a baseball player, boxing champion, the President, or some military hero. Obviously, this is not an adequate substitute for the warm, personal relationship with an older man near at hand that is so sorely needed at this time.

Even if Jimmie is fortunate enough to have such a relationship with his father or another man, he is likely to go through a difficult time. His need for reassurance and ever more reassurance is the basis of his close friendship with one other boy. This type of fraternization is typical of adolescence.

Jimmie and his special friend Pete are inseparable. They walk to and from school together arm in arm, or with their arms flung across each other's shoulders. They spend long hours together behind closed doors, looking at pornographic pictures, tracking down terms in the dictionary and encyclopedia. They are afraid of sex and yet eager to know about it. They confide in each other and discover with great relief that they have the same secret thoughts and phantasies.

Remember your boyhood friend Tom or Dick or whatever his name was? Remember how you were chums—pals—cronies —buddies? The word is different according to when you were a boy, but the relationship is the same. It is rooted in a basic need and it is entirely natural.

It is also entirely natural for two boys to examine each other's genitals, to engage in mutual masturbation and induce emissions. This experience may produce such feelings of guilt that their friendship is broken. It may make them feel closer, and it may lead to subsequent similar experiences.

Such physical relationships are frequent among boys at camp or boarding school, where all of them are separated from their families and are lonely. There is ample opportunity for a boy to creep into another boy's bed. The body contact excites them both. They hold each other closely, get great satisfaction from skin contact, and they may kiss. Very likely, mutual masturbation follows. The boy who lives at home may also have such experiences. Yet all boys, obviously, do not desire them or indeed need them.

Many of the games of adolescence are substitutes for actual homosexual activities. When two boys wrestle and pummel each other, each attempts to "prove his masculinity" by pinning the other one down. They fall on top of each other in various grotesque positions. Sometimes a group of boys gang up on one lad, throw him to the ground and pile up on him. The longer they can maintain their precarious balance, face downward on top of the victim, the better is the sport. In such roughhousing, and more clearly in the many variations of "Church on Fire" and "Johnny on the Pony," the boys are enjoying a homosexual contact, although they may not be aware of what they are doing. These actions are natural. The point cannot be stressed too often.

The period from ten to fifteen years of age, roughly speaking, is a homosexual phase. Do not be afraid of accepting the idea or of using the term. It will normally be outgrown. Mutual masturbation and overt homosexual activities of this period may be thought of as rehearsals for a later, heterosexual relationship, although they do not in any way make that relationship more successful. In essence the two things are entirely different. The boys must carry on their homosexual contacts furtively, and they are well aware that they are doing something that is disapproved by society, especially by their parents. Thus there is guilt and anxiety. The satisfaction of physical drives that is provided by the true sex act is lacking. More important, the element of tenderness, so essential for complete adult heterosexual satisfaction, is absent. If all goes well, as it usually does, the homosexual phase will recede, and heterosexual development will show itself, first in general interest in girls, then in attachment to one girl and finally in successful marriage.

These feelings and events, however, come later on.

Let us look more closely at Jimmie and his comrades in this first phase of adolescence. Foremost among their interests is generally school, with its many scholastic and extracurricular activities. The way in which the boys react in this sphere tells us a great deal about their personalities, and about whether they have passed normally through the phases of infancy and childhood or have been unduly fixated at some one phase.

Sam is perpetually worried about his schoolwork. In the evening, even before he starts his homework, he is sure it will be all wrong. He pictures himself in class the next day, with the teacher scolding him for not knowing his lessons, and he cannot sleep. On the way to school the next morning, his worry increases and is almost too much to bear. He hates school, the teachers and the world in general. Finally the moment arrives for turning in his homework. It is correct, and the teacher praises him in class. But this happy outcome solves nothing. The next evening, and the next, and the next, he is in the same squirrel cage of worry and anxiety. Although the papers he turns in are perfect, day after day, he is sure that the next one he does will be full of mistakes. What is the matter with Sam, that he can learn nothing from experience? He is fearful that if he makes a mistake no one will love him. And this fear is a carry-over from the late oral phase of his infancy when he first came face to face with the fear of being abandoned by his mother. For some reason he has kept too many of the characteristics of this phase, instead of dropping them as he passed on to later phases.

Philip also cannot learn from experience, but his difficulty comes from having retained too many of the traits of the Anal Phase, the period of habit formation. Philip applies himself meticulously to his homework. His notebooks are marvels of orderliness, and day after day he does well in class. Yet he is doubtful of his capacities. He makes no attempts to be friendly with his classmates and has no time for out-of-school activities. The term for a person with Philip's personality traits is "perfectionist." He is uncertain about what is the best course to follow, doubtful of the outcome of whatever he does. As a result, he suffers from anxiety and needs constant reassurance; he also procrastinates, postponing any action lest it be the wrong thing to do.

The perfectionist lives through every experience twice—during the stage of planning and during its actual occurrence. No task is a pleasure; it is a ritual, painstakingly carried out to the smallest detail. To avoid the failure that he is sure will occur, the perfectionist seeks some avenue of escape. He may get sick—vomit or have diarrhea. The rejection of food, it is interesting to note, is a "displacement" of the psychological rejection of a situation. The perfectionist has a strong sense of righteousness. He expects everyone else to behave as he does, and is irritable and upset if they do not do so, and if their actions thwart him in having everything "just so."

Another lad, Harry, has moved successfully through the early developmental phases, but he has retained to too great a degree the traits of the phallic phase. He is spurred on at school by envy and an overwhelming urge to compete with his comrades. He asserts himself in class, and is aggressive and cocksure. He must stand out from the other students and be better than they are in everything—academic and athletic. Harry really feels inferior to his schoolmates, and he hides this feeling by acting superior to them. He attaches himself to the good students and gets along if he is their equal intellectually. If he falls short of their standards and they do not accept him as one of the crowd, he may take refuge in razzing.

And then there is Robert, or shall we say "Bing"? His ambivalence takes the form of complete cleavage between the kind of person he is at home and at school. Robert to his family; Bing to his schoolmates. A terror at home; well-behaved and disciplined at school. The explanation of his behavior is simple, although the solution of the difficulty is complex. Robert-Bing has accepted authority at school, but at home he is still acting out the role of the all-powerful baby who cries and gets his way during the oral or narcissistic phase.

You will see from these few examples, I hope, how an understanding of the successive phases of development and their salient characteristics will help you understand your adolescent son. You will recognize that he is still an immature individual, whose emotional development does not precisely coincide with his chronological age. This viewpoint will keep you from blaming him when he does not live up to your ideal of an all-round, easily functioning lad.

Aside from the problems of personality fixations, school gives rise to difficulties for any adolescent boy. The teacher, if a woman, must be accepted as "authority" for part of the time, in place of the former authority of the mother. If the teacher is a man, as is fortunately the case in many of the upper school grades, he is in a sense a substitute father and his personality has a profound effect on the boy's progress and on his later relationships with other men. A kind, understanding male teacher may help the boy overcome whatever resistance he has toward his own father. A harsh and strict teacher may strengthen that resistance. Competition, with all its tensions, is inevitable—competition with classmates, with brothers and sisters, with cousins and neighbors. And sometimes parents unwisely put too much pressure on their son during this period in their effort to have him do well at school.

I pointed out at the opening of this chapter that curiosity was one of the adolescent's chief characteristics. In the out-of-school half of Jimmie's life, his insatiable curiosity, his many unrelated interests, his need to know about "everything" also make for pressures and confusion. How on earth is he to find time for baseball and football, movies, music lessons, reading, club meetings, radio and TV programs, the carpentry "business" he and his friend have started, hikes, taxidermy and so on and so on? How can he possibly do all these things and still do his household chores, take the dratted baths he is supposed to take, keep himself and his clothes and his room neat and clean?

In all these activities, as in his school life, the traits of the adolescent's earlier years show up. This is seen particularly clearly in athletics. One boy may be highly competitive, determined to beat his opponent. He may succumb to tricks and dishonesty to win, or he may defeat himself, as it were—tripping as he reaches the final tape or having some other sort of "accident." Then everyone tells him he would have won—tough luck, and that sort of thing. He has managed to escape the final showdown and yet be acclaimed. Another, better adjusted, will do his best, keep to the rules of the game, and accept the outcome—be it victory or defeat—with good grace and sportsmanship. He will also function well in team activities, acting as the leader or accepting the leadership of another boy, as the case may be. He has a sense of camaraderie and of loyalty to the group, and the emotional satisfaction that comes from thinking in terms of "all for one and one for all."

Not all boys, of course, participate in athletic events. Many are spectators, but as such they are by no means passive. They get as excited as though they were shooting the basket or rushing the ball down the field. Through identification, they play the game with their comrades who are actually in the scrap.

Identification also accounts in large part for the adolescent's tense interest in the movies. He projects himself into the picture, and what happens is happening to *him*. In moments of excitement he bites his nails, tugs at his genitals and perhaps wets his pants. He is the hero, cruising in his private yacht, riding the range, shooting down the gangsters. Radio, too, fills the needs of this period. Almost all parents of adolescents complain about how their youngsters keep the radio turned on continuously, how they study, read, dress, and sometimes even sleep with the radio turned on full blast. They somehow manage to take in what is going on without paying too much attention. They also seem to like the sound, quite aside from the sense. This sound is, as it were, the substitute for the ever-present adult—mother or baby sitter—of childhood.

TV programs are rapidly gaining favor with adolescents at the expense of radio or even the movies. The effect of this relatively new medium has not yet been clearly determined. We do know that it takes up a lot of the adolescent's time, interferes with homework and reading, and is often preferred to many other activities. We know, too, that identification is part of its appeal. Much of the adolescent's aggression—about which I shall talk soon—is harmlessly drawn off as he identifies himself with the slapstick comedians, the boxers and especially the wrestlers who appear on TV.

Jimmie and his comrades at this stage of adolescence are generally collectors of stamps, coins, autographs, pictures of baseball or football players or of movie stars. Some lads seem to be obsessed by collecting, devoting every spare moment to it; others take it in stride, as one of many things that interest them; and still others soon outgrow this hobby. While the "collection fever" lasts, each lad wants to have as good a collection as his comrades, or a better one, for this gives him prestige and helps him feel secure.

Jimmie's eager-beaver activities and his spurts of bravado often make us lose sight of the fact that he is insecure and whistling in the dark much of the time at this bewildering part of his journey through life. His childhood acceptance of his parents as all-wise, all-good and all-knowing is crumbling, and he is beginning to see them objectively and probably beginning to note undesirable traits and qualities. Dad especially is in for critical scrutiny. He is no longer the pillar of strength and power, the envied one of earlier years. His hair is probably getting gray or falling out, he has a slight stoop and perhaps a paunch, his tennis is pretty poor and he puffs when he walks fast. Jimmie, on the other hand, has become taller, heavier and more muscular. By gosh, he can do a lot of things Dad can't do, he knows a lot of things Dad doesn't know. Jimmie is breaking away from his father's authority. He delights in trapping Dad with questions he is well aware his father can't answer, and he parades pat solutions for world problems. Confirming his present feeling that Dad is not omnipotent, he tries out his own power to the hilt. Certainly Dad can no longer punish him physically; he could lick Dad with one hand behind his back. So he tests his father's ability—or any other adult's ability—to control him. This is the basic mechanism of the adolescent's aggression and vandalism. This is, in a nutshell, why he breaks things, marks up cars with chalk, lets air out of tires, dumps over garbage cans and takes particular delight in breaking windows with popguns or stones.

The battle for power is not limited to the destruction of physical things. Jimmie, now convinced that he is stronger in every way than his father, turns to some cause or "public leader." He wants to champion the underdog, to be a protester, at war with all authority.

This is natural and as it should be. If you understand what is happening to Jimmie, you will not be upset or hurt at his flare-ups and criticism, his rebellious outbursts, his so-called impertinence. You will realize that he has a need at this time to challenge, and indeed defy, authority. And you will go very slow in your attempts to control and train him in the same way as you did when he was a small boy.

One of the chief bones of contention between parents and their adolescent boy is smoking. In his eagerness to be a man, Jimmie feels compelled to take on the habits of men and to act like men. An obvious way of doing this is to smoke. You can lay down rules forbidding Jimmie to smoke until he is, let us say, eighteen, and punish him when he breaks the rules, but he will smoke all the same. He will smoke on the sly, away from home, partly to "show you" and to prove to himself that he's no longer under your thumb, and partly for other and complex reasons.

Smoking, as the cigarette advertising copy writers know, gives one a feeling of comfort and coziness. Think of the slogans—They Satisfy—Smooth. They indicate pleasure of a particular kind, the kind that the nursing infant feels, sucking at his mother's breast, that the child feels, sucking his thumb, a lollipop, and later, an ice cream cone. The pipe, with its stem that fits so snugly into the mouth and with its warm bowl, the cigarette and cigar with their soft tips, are something to hold onto, something that unconsciously are symbols of the mother of infancy. So, they mean comfort and security and well-being.

This feeling is deep-seated. Two men, when they get together to iron out some disagreement, will generally first go through the ritual of offering each other a cigarette, a light, and so on, and "light up" and puff for a few moments. Then, with hostility and rivalry somewhat abated, they will begin to discuss the matter at hand. The Indian, you will recall, smoked a peace pipe with his former enemy as a sign that they were henceforth to be friends.

Much has been said and written about how smoking stunts a youth's growth, diminishes his lung capacity, and makes him susceptible to tuberculosis or cancer of the lungs. These statements have no basis in fact, and they should not be used as arguments to keep an adolescent from smoking. The facts indicate that smoking is not harmful in early youth but may be harmful in later life. The nicotine in tobacco tends to constrict

the arteries. In youth the circulatory system is flexible and col-
lateral circulation is readily established. Theoretically, after the
age of thirty, with progressive loss of flexibility and the thicken-
ing and hardening of the arteries, the effects of nicotine cannot
so readily be nullified. As to the danger of cancer of the lungs
being induced by smoking, let us look at the facts. At the turn
of the century, cancer of the lungs was found chiefly in men in
the age group forty-five to sixty, with a comparatively small
number of cases in younger people. Since that time, smoking
by men and women of all ages has increased steadily. Lung
cancer has also increased, but it occurs predominantly in men
between the ages of forty-five and fifty, not in younger men.
It has been found that the majority of the victims have been
continuous chain smokers over many years, and that a significantly small number are men who were excessive smokers during early adulthood but subsequently gave up or modified the
habit.

These facts support my attitude about smoking. If you give
the adolescent the satisfaction of smoking, by the time he is
thirty he will generally stop entirely or modify the habit to
such an extent that it no longer constitutes a danger in induc-
ing lung cancer. I raise this point to emphasize that it is unwise
as well as futile for the parents of an adolescent to "forbid
him to smoke." To do so on the basis of physical health is un-
founded. To do so for other reasons flies in the face of deep-
rooted urges, makes an issue where there need be none. Perhaps parents are themselves in emotional conflict, since acceptance of the fact that their son is approaching manhood means
that they must also accept the fact that they themselves are
growing old. To put the matter in its simplest terms, Jimmie
gets a sense of well-being and security from smoking; it re-
minds him of the warmth and love he had as an infant and
child. Let him smoke and enjoy himself.

If parents have been understanding and flexible during this stormy period of early adolescence, the chances are that Jimmie as he approaches his fifteenth year, or thereabouts, is feeling less hostile and rebellious. He has gained some sort of position among his comrades through athletics or other activities, and he has learned through his skirmishes with his father that he must, somehow, live with his family and accept a measure of parental authority until he is older. He is beginning to get a clearer idea of his own personality, his aptitudes and weaknesses.

With his primary guilt feelings about his phantasies during masturbation somewhat lessened, he turns again to his mother and seeks her affection and attention. It is a short step from this feeling to interest in girls, after his almost exclusive focus on boys. And again, a short step from general interest in girls and awareness of their attractiveness to the singling out of some one girl.

To gain her attention, Jimmie must make himself attractive. His habits about his clothes and his person change drastically. Dungarees and T-shirts or whatever the gang usually wears, no longer suffice. For his "date," Jimmie must have a suit, he must put on a nice clean shirt and a tie, polish his shoes, scrub his nails, slick down his hair. To dress up makes him feel more important. He is a clean, presentable young man —at least he tries to be—and the girls in his class at school and in the neighborhood notice him and invite him to their parties. Even more important, his particular girl notices him. But he goes back to dungarees, of course, for the approval of other boys is also important to him and he does not want to be thought a sissy.

Since most parties are given by girls, I shall postpone describing them and what role they play in Jimmie's life until the next chapter which deals with Sally during her early adolescence, and speak here only about Jimmie and his special girl. Adults shrug off "puppy love" as of no importance or as something to joke about, but it is a serious business for Jimmie. His daydreams, formerly concerned almost exclusively with crime, adventure, and his own physical or perhaps financial prowess, now include lovemaking, marriage, the honeymoon, the home he will have and the children he will enjoy. His phantasies are grandiose and unrelated to reality. He will have a vast estate, not a small house or apartment; he and his wife will take a trip around the world for their honeymoon; no week at Niagara Falls for them. He will have exactly the number of children his fancy dictates, of the desired sex and looks, and he will provide them with everything he lacked in his own childhood. The future looks bright. He will be happy and whatever he wishes for will come true.

Family kidding about Jimmie and his girl is a thorn in his side, and many a dinner table flare-up is touched off when a younger brother or sister, or even one of the parents, gives a burlesqued report of what the pair said to each other during their interminable telephone conversations. Parents often think that a lad is too young to be "in love" and unwisely tell him so. Actually, he will be in love when he has attained the necessary psychological development for heterosexual adjustment. No one can say when this time arrives in terms of calendar years. Meanwhile do not belittle "puppy love." It is an important milestone in your son's life.

As a squire to his girl, Jimmie comes smack up against the problem of money. Up to this time his allowance has seemed fairly adequate for his needs, and it has been spent pretty much as his mother dictates—so much for carfare, so much for school lunches, for movies, for afterschool ice cream, and (let us hope) enough left over to treat to ice cream cones when it is necessary to stand in well or be especially important with the gang.

Now he needs money for his "dates," and he doesn't want to explain just how it is to be spent. So he may resort to subterfuge and report additional expenses for lunches or school supplies in an effort to get his allowance raised. He may meet his financial problem by foregoing his daily ice cream and by skimping in other ways in order to accumulate enough money to take his girl to the movies, with whatever trimmings are customary in his set.

Jimmie has begun to realize the importance of money and what money can buy. He will pattern himself on his parents in handling it, and be frugal or spendthrift—or strike a happy mean between extremes—according to their habits. At this stage in his development his parents should include him in the family councils about finances and should let him make suggestions. An awareness of the family's financial setup and problems, and participation in their solution will be a rehearsal for the adult role he is getting ready to play; they will help him later on in planning his future.

By the time Jimmie is about fifteen, he has developed a fair inner control. He is no longer concerned only with himself. He realizes that he must be aware of other people's needs and must adjust to them. He perceives that one cannot be a child and an adult at one and the same time, and so he has overcome much of his indecision about these two roles and some of his ambivalence.

The question naturally arises, *why* does Jimmie change in this way? During this period he gradually finds that earlier childhood habits no longer serve their purposes. He has the opportunity of absorbing the attitudes of those around him, and he begins to recognize how adults function. Through his intellectual development he has learned to think for himself instead of leaning on the opinions of others. He has grown physically, and his external appearance is now more manly; as a result, people treat him as a man, and he tries to live up to their attitude.

In sum, a new element has been added to—or rather superimposed on—the psychological structure of the formative years. Jimmie's personality is now a combination of the developmental process of the formative years and the effects of the environment. This statement—oversimplified, I am well aware—explains why Jimmie is no longer entirely concerned with himself, why he is becoming aware of others and beginning to learn how to adjust to others.

CHAPTER THREE

Girls Will Become Women

Early Adolescence

YOUR ADOLESCENT DAUGHTER is very much like your adolescent son—and yet very different. Like him, she is contradictory, unpredictable and confused. Ambivalence is the key to her bewildering behavior, as it is the key to his. But her reactions to the complexities of adolescence, her responses to the crosscurrents of this period of her development are not identical with those of a boy.

Your young daughter is reluctant to leave childhood, yet eager to enter womanhood. And because she seems to know intuitively that womanhood will be for her both a time of great joy and a time of great responsibility, her reluctance and her eagerness are deeper and more emotional than the adolescent boy's. This is one of the chief differences between the two.

The well-known lines of Longfellow's poem *Maidenhood* come to mind when we think of any adolescent girl. This is how he describes her:

> Standing with reluctant feet,
> Where the brook and river meet,
> Womanhood and childhood fleet!
> Gazing, with a timid glance
> On the brooklet's swift advance,
> On the river's broad expanse.
> Then why pause with indecision . . .

Sally's indecision, she knows deep down inside, is futile. Inevitably she will be carried out onto the river's broad expanse, and life will see to it that she is a woman, not a little girl playing at womanhood, as some men seem to "get away with" being small boys well on into middle age. Nevertheless, she makes one final protest when the bodily changes that mark the beginning of adolescence appear. It is as if she clings, for one last moment, to childhood.

Jimmie, you will recall, is proud of the first faint signs of hair on his face and boasts to his cronies about this and other indications that he will soon be a man. Sally reacts quite differently to the physical signs that are the prelude to womanhood. Her breasts are developing, her arms and legs are getting longer and slimmer, her round baby face is "thinning down." She is self-conscious, bashful and ashamed. Suddenly she wants privacy; no one, not even Mother, must see her dress and undress, or come into the bathroom while she is taking a bath. By not letting anyone see her, she can perhaps not "see herself," can make believe that nothing is different. Thus she tries to deny the evidence of her own eyes, to hold back the sands of time. She changes abruptly from a talkative happy child to a silent withdrawn girl, depressed and readily moved to tears. Sally is unconsciously mourning the loss of her carefree childhood. Without actually knowing it, she is anxious and doubtful about the advantages of the woman's role that she must inevitably accept.

In her effort to deny what is happening, Sally is likely to become a tomboy, to play along with the boys in their roughest games, wear dungarees and a boy's shirt—probably with the tails dangling outside—socks and sloppy saddle shoes. For a time she is unwilling to accept the idea that she is becoming a woman and yet knows that she cannot remain a child; so she seems to try to find a way out by trying to become a boy.

This period of denial, however, is brief. Sally's feminine instinct asserts itself, the instinct for attracting males that all females—human and animal alike—possess. Taking her cue from older girls, Sally soon begins to accept her female role. She drops her tomboy ways and tries to look her best in order to be attractive.

As is the case with boys, the first indications of a girl's adolescence do not come at a fixed age. The range in years for its onset is wide, as it is for boys. Sally may stand where the brook and river meet as early as her ninth year, or as late as her fifteenth, or anywhere in between. Mothers are apt to think their daughters are having an "early" adolescence or a "late" adolescence, meaning that the time is different from what they expected it to be in the light of their own experience. It is far better to keep in mind that girls will enter adolescence when the time—for each individual—is at hand, and to accept that time as normal. The bodily changes, whenever they occur, will usher in the emotional changes.

Like Jimmie, Sally is filled with curiosity about life. Like him, she has a great and urgent, an almost insatiable need to know about the world. Her interest, however, is in people rather than things, in feelings and situations, rather than in facts. She and her girl friends talk endlessly about what happens to people, actual and imaginary, about what kind of men they will fall in love with and marry, about their children-to-be, and about older girls and their conquests and difficulties with boys.

Sally tries to find out about life by examining it in books, in other people, and first and foremost in herself—her body, with its signs of approaching womanhood, her thoughts and phantasies. For these enterprises she needs privacy, and it is to be hoped that she will have a room of her own. There she can be safe from loving—and prying—eyes and satisfy her almost passionate desire to be alone. Part of this desire comes from modesty, the unconscious wish to hide from others—and herself—the signs of bodily change, as I have explained above. Part of it is just the opposite. She wants to think about these changes, to play out various roles that belong to women—the passionate mistress, the pregnant wife, the temptress alluring and invincible, the young mother. She takes these roles in phantasy and in actuality, striding about her room in improvised costumes, talking to herself.

Probably Sally keeps a diary, just as Jimmie does. But unlike her brother, she does not use it to recount imaginary deeds of prowess and as a means of talking back to parents and teachers. Her diary is her confidante. It is the ever-ready listener, to which she can tell the romantic things—imaginary for the most part—that happen to her. Some attractive and prominent boy at school is perhaps the hero. Although in actuality he and Sally have never talked together or have only the most casual contact, in her diary she sets down a continued story (a veritable soap opera) of her experiences with this boy, the unfolding of their love, how they are separated and blissfully reunited, how she rejects him, or more likely how he rejects her. Sometimes the hero of these diary stories, in which of course Sally is the heroine, is a popular movie actor or some man in the public eye.

Sometimes a difficult home situation is the start of her phantasy tale. She records in her diary that she is an outcast, perhaps a foundling, and that her real parents are of noble birth. Her need to be loved is so great that she imagines—and often recounts—how many men love her, how she is perhaps a prostitute, prowling the dark streets at night, holding a position of power in the underworld, or mistreated by the police, enslaved by one cruel and attractive man.

Whatever the tales that are spun by Sally's vivid adolescent imagination, they all show not only her need to be loved but also her instinctive need to inflict pain and punishment upon herself. She has phantasies of rape, of cruelty and anguish and self-effacement. And she also has phantasies of being admired and adored, of being decked with glittering jewels and costly furs by the man who worships her, of graciously letting her lover kiss her finger tips, or of swooning under his ardent kisses.

In addition to her diary Sally usually has a close friendship with another girl of her own age, somewhat like the special friendship between Jimmie and his pal. The girls' relationship, however, has more emotional content than the boys', and is generally not a physical relationship.

Sally and her "best friend" will act out some of the things that they have each been confiding to their diaries. They carry on a sort of continuous theatrical performance, with themselves as actors, authors, and audience. Frequently, they will act out the role of pregnancy, stuffing pillows under their dresses, walking in a sluggish, dragging fashion, pushing away imaginary food and speaking in whispers. Although they have seen their mothers or other women behave normally and happily during pregnancy, they seem to enjoy dwelling on all the difficulties of pregnancy. They have heard that "labor pains" are to be expected and must be endured by women.

The two girls will also act out the role of prostitutes, as they recount past experiences and make plans for future conquests, talking tough and walking around the room in a tough gait. Such play acting and other sexual phantasies rarely carry over into actuality. There is much discussion of each other's looks and good and bad points, their "oomph" or "it" or whatever the current slang is for sexual attractiveness. The two girls rarely, however, actually examine each other to compare their physical development. In this respect they differ from boys in the same phase of adolescence. In boys the homosexual aspect of the twosome is fairly open; in girls it is veiled and the relationship is emotional, not physical. Sally and her friend have "secrets" so complex and intricate that no mere adult could hope to understand them.

In their confused state of fear and eagerness about growing up, they draw comfort from a sense of togetherness and affection for each other. They talk endlessly about sex and courtship and marriage, things they are obviously not yet ready for, and they demand from each other loyalty and single-minded devotion such as they may some day give and receive from a man. The intrusion of a third girl into this safe, warm partnership arouses jealousy and anger incomprehensible to an outsider. Tricks of fearful and wonderful intricacy are set in motion to find out "who said what to whom," and if it turns out that confidences have been betrayed, if Sally finds out that Jane has been "disloyal" to her, their friendship may break up, and each one will find another best friend.

As a rule, after a brief period of twosome partnerships, each girl turns once more to her mother. You will recall that Jimmie wants to be close to his father or some man who can take his father's place during this phase of adolescence. Sally likewise feels the need for a close relationship with her mother or a mother substitute.

Intimacy between mother and daughter is perhaps more easily achieved than intimacy between father and son. Dad may talk with Bill, play games and go on hikes with him, work with him in the basement carpentry shop, but when he goes to work Bill cannot readily follow him even in imagination. He is lost in that mysterious office or shop or factory. But Sally can see what her mother does when she is at work, and she can also work with her. She watches and helps her mother market and cook, clean the house, do the wash and take care of the younger children. She knows that she will herself be doing these things when she becomes a woman. Thus she has a definite pattern to follow and to imitate. As the psychologists put it, she can identify herself with her mother.

This situation makes it easier for a mother to tell her daughter about menstruation, that major bodily change that generally comes soon after the first manifestations of adolescence. Just as a boy should be prepared for nocturnal emissions before he actually experiences them, a girl should be prepared for her first menstruation before it appears. When this is not done, she will be ashamed and shocked by the unusual event.

The mother should explain the physiological basis of menstruation and should make clear that it is a normal and natural function. She has a grave responsibility, for her own attitude toward menstruation will have a great affect on her daughter's. The attitude of other women and older girls will also affect her, but less strongly.

If Sally hears the girls and women around her, particularly her mother, complain of headaches, dizziness, nausea, and cramps, she will expect that she too will suffer from these ailments when she menstruates. And in all likelihood she *will*. If she sees her mother give way to irritability and emotional upsets, and plead menstruation as an excuse, she will very probably also use this excuse for not keeping her emotions under control.

The various names used for this normal bodily function—unwell, sick, the curse, red flag, monthlies, woman's troubles—suggest that it is something dirty and unpleasant, something that everyone would avoid if it were possible to do so. The adolescent takes her cue from her mother and older girls.

"I'm not feeling so good, it's my sick time," Sally's mother says. "I've got a headache—I'm nervous—cranky—I really can't play bridge tonight—I don't want to go to the movies."

Small wonder that Sally, in turn, not only pleads a headache and backache and cramps to get out of doing something she doesn't want to do during her menstrual period; she actually does have that headache and backache and cramps. She just "has to" go to bed.

The endocrine changes attendant upon menstruation may result in heightened sensitivity, irritability and some instability of mood, but not, it should be emphasized, to the extent that they cannot be controlled. The healthy, normal girl who has not been set a bad example by her elders, especially her mother, should be free from physical discomfort and able to control whatever emotional stress she has during her menstrual period. The abnormal effects of menstruation in a healthy normal girl are entirely the result of the attitude of those around her. Age-old taboos about not touching flowers, lest they die, and not making jelly because it will spoil should be recognized as old wives' tales that have no place in modern life. Likewise the old-fashioned idea that a girl must not bathe or dance or take any kind of exercise while menstruating should be scotched. She can continue to carry on all her usual activities, including swimming and dancing. These points need to be stressed again and again. They need to be fully understood and accepted by the parents of adolescent girls and indeed by all who are in contact with these girls.

Up to a generation ago the mechanics of menstruation, it must be confessed, made it difficult for a girl or woman to feel or act "normally." The "telltale" pads were ever in her mind. The chafing made it difficult to exercise and swimming was, of course, out of the question. Today we have cylindrical pads of absorbent material which can be inserted into the vagina during the menstrual period. They remain snugly in place, with no external indication that they are there, absorb the flow, eliminate telltale odors and protuberances.

It may be protested that the hymen, symbol of virginity, must be broken in order to introduce this vaginal pad. In reply I say that the hymen serves no useful purpose. The badge of virginity should be the girl's conscience, rather than a meaningless symbol. Moreover, the breaking of the hymen before marriage eliminates the disastrous anxiety of the nuptial night. With the vaginal canal already open, the first experience of sexual intercourse is not a painful task but a mutual pleasure.

The close relationship that develops between mother and daughter has in it the seeds of discord. When Sally hears from her mother about menstruation, she may be resentful because this "secret" has been kept from her up to this time. Her resentment is even stronger if her mother tells her nothing about menstruation but lets her find out about it from other girls. In any case she is likely to wonder and brood about whether her mother, despite her outward show of frankness, is keeping other "secrets" from her. Knowing by this time about sexual intercourse, she begins to think, perhaps so deep down that she is hardly aware of it, about her mother's sex life and the relations between her mother and father.

She has feelings of animosity toward her mother—perhaps she is jealous of her as the queen bee, the foremost woman in the family circle. And yet she loves her mother and has a deep affection for her. As in other aspects of adolescence, Sally is ambivalent in her feelings toward her mother. She fluctuates between intimacy and aloofness, secretiveness and frankness. Fortunate the girl whose mother understands these changes of attitude and mood and can take them in her stride without resentment.

And here we touch on an added complication in the relationship between the adolescent girl and her mother. How the mother reacts to her daughter will depend largely on the kind of person she herself is. This is not as simple an idea as it appears to be. You will recall that some persons are "fixated" at some stage of their early development. If the mother is still caught fast at the oral, narcissistic stage, and demands continuous affection and attention from all around her, she will not want to share the limelight with her young daughter. She will feel jealous and antagonistic, but she would probably be shocked if you put her feelings into words.

One day Mrs. Brown was talking to me about her sixteen-year-old daughter Betty. She complained bitterly how Betty kept the house in a turmoil with her friends flocking in and out at all hours, her endless talking on the telephone, her demands for new dance frocks, and so on.

"Perhaps you're jealous of her," I said quietly, when she paused for breath. "Perhaps you'd like to be the young lady of the household instead of fortyish and losing your figure if not your looks."

"Why—why, the very idea," she sputtered. "I just love Betty. I want her to have a good time—I'm happy that she's so pretty."

Perfectly true. And yet the opposite is true, too. Mrs. Brown, because she hadn't really grown up—remember, her actual age had nothing to do with the situation—was ambivalent, just as her daughter was ambivalent. The difference, and it is an important one, is that in adolescents, ambivalence is natural and to be expected, but in grownups it is unnatural and is a sign that they have not won their way through to adulthood.

With the coming of menstruation, the young girl seems to accept her feminine role, she is happy about all the signs of approaching womanhood, and her attempts to look and act like a boy recede into the background. She watches those around her—older girls at school, teachers and camp councillors, heroines of stage and screen, and tries to copy their attractive traits. She studies how they dress and walk, how they do their hair and put on their make-up, how they speak and act. From each one she takes whatever seems to her to be desirable.

This is why Sally will talk like Elizabeth Taylor one week, and like Julie Harris the next. Why she brushes her hair flat to her head and puts on a Mona Lisa smile, and then crops her hair close, all over curls, and grins like the girl who is "in love with a wonderful guy." Why she demands severe tailored clothes today, and wants frivolous ones, all lace and ruffles, tomorrow. She is taking a bit of this and a bit of that from those around her, she is experimenting. Keeping and discarding, she is attempting to build up—or rather to find—the personality that she will carry on into womanhood.

In preparation for what now seems to her a desirable future, she takes great care of her body, trying to make it beautiful. She watches her diet, to be thin or curved as the fashion is, but never fat. She exercises, following with keen interest directions for developing shapely legs or avoiding sway-back. She spends an unbelievable amount of time on facials and baths and manicures, and her desire for cosmetics and perfumes appears to be insatiable.

Sally's interest in herself helps her develop self-assurance. She is no longer the reticent shy girl of a year ago. She seems to feel that she knows more than anyone else, and that what she says should be listened to with respect. Her close identification with her mother wanes, as she slowly but surely makes a personality pattern for herself. Often she is quite critical of her mother and of how things are done at home, and offers sweeping and arbitrary plans for changes in furnishings, in food, and other household arrangements. If her suggestions are not swiftly carried out—and obviously they generally are not— Sally is hurt and angry.

Unconsciously she is testing her parents' love, particularly her mother's, by making demands that she knows, deep down, cannot be granted. Let me make clear that parents are under no compulsion to "give in" to their adolescent daughter. If they do, she will only put up a higher hurdle, make a more preposterous demand. She *wants* to be at odds with her family, for she is trying to free herself from close family ties. Almost anything will serve as justification for what she needs to do at this stage.

"We've just got to get a new dining room set," Sally blurts out at dinner one evening. "This one is hopelessly old-fashioned, and I'm just ashamed of the way the room looks."

Useless to counter that the set was bought two years ago, or that the family budget won't run to a new one, or that everyone else in the family likes it. Sally isn't playing this hand on the level of reason.

"I wish you could see the dining room at Rosalind's house," she says. "Everything there is so lovely."

This is the crux of the matter. Everything somewhere that isn't home is "lovely," not because it actually is nicer but because the time has come for Sally to turn her eyes from home, to focus her interests and affections on someone outside of the family.

She helps herself do this, as it were, by dwelling on her mother's shortcomings, by finding fault with things at home and so justifying her interest in someone outside of the family circle. Most frequently she develops a "crush," as it is called, on a teacher, and tries to establish a close emotional relationship with her. Sometimes the teacher is not responsive. Sally, since she has a great need for love and attention, will then turn to some older girl. A relationship between the two develops that has many of the elements of a man-woman attachment. There is love and mutual protection, hostility and jealousy, sentimental attachment and unselfish concern. The relationship is homoerotic, that is, a reflection of self-love, but there is very little body contact beyond holding hands, kissing, and perhaps sleeping together. Even when the two girls lie in bed together, there is usually no sexual play.

Adolescent girls differ in this respect from adolescent boys. Their greater emotional capacity seems to make it unnecessary for them to experiment in physical sex. They appear not to need the intermediate step of homosexual relations before they have the experience of adult heterosexual life. Through phantasy and concepts of romance they are able to prepare themselves for what lies ahead. To dream about sex, to seek and win affection, call it love if you will, from another girl is enough.

This phase of adolescence serves a useful purpose. Sally, in her close and emotional relationship with another girl or woman, learns to develop a feeling for someone besides herself. She is quick to notice minor changes in mood in her friend, and thus she becomes sensitive to the feelings of another person. She is able to understand her friend's emotions and behavior, and to "project herself" into her friend's feelings.

This quality is called empathy. It is a valuable and endearing trait, something that makes us "take to another person," feel at home with her, confide in her. When a person has empathy we know, intuitively, that she will understand us and be helpful and loyal.

Sally's emotional concern for her friend widens out into emotional concern for all human beings who are suffering, and indeed for animals that need love and care. Every situation is assessed on a personal basis, on how she would feel and want someone to behave were she in this poor sick old woman's shoes—or were she this poor deserted dog or cat.

As Sally is developing empathy she is also developing a capacity to size up situations, to understand how and why other people act as they do. She is, we may say, beginning to exercise her intuition, one of the fundamental feminine characteristics.

You will recall that Jimmie, in the comparable phase of his development, is not much interested in his mother, but wants to be close to his father. This situation is not quite the reverse for Sally. Her small-girl affection for Daddy is carried over into adolescence and she never feels separated from him. She still likes to roughhouse with Daddy, to jump on him and make him take a lot of "punishment"; she likes to let him hurt her—almost—in acrobatic stunts. In some ways, however, things are different from what they were a few years ago. Sally is taller and heavier, for one thing, and Daddy is probably unable to lift her up on his shoulders and carry her around on his back. Then, too, he appears to be unwilling to wrestle with her as he used to do. Sally is vaguely aware of the sexual excitation in all this cutting up, and senses that she "likes" to be hurt by Daddy—both physically and emotionally. The technical term for the former feeling is eroticism, and for the latter, masochism. Both are present in the young adolescent girl. Because she has these feelings, Sally has a sense of guilt, of uneasiness and discomfort in close physical proximity with Daddy. Thus the stage is set for her to turn from him to boys, just as Jimmie turns his attention to girls.

School and out-of-school activities, of course, bring girls and boys into close contact, but their major get-togethers are at parties. These social gatherings begin in childhood and change in character as the participants pass through the various phases of development. It is worth while to see what parties are like in this period of adolescence, for they are a clue to the young people's needs.

A group of about six boys and six girls is usually invited to the home of one of the girls, for it is the girls who give the parties. Generally they prefer to meet in front of the house and enter as a group, to avoid the embarrassment of greeting the hostess's mother or both parents individually. At first, all the guests are self-conscious. The girls cluster together, or help set the table and bring out the food. The party in its early stages revolves around eating, just as children's parties do. Pretzels, peanuts, and potato chips are stand-bys, along with cold meats, cake and fruit. No fancy sandwiches or canapés are tolerated. Soft drinks are offered. At first everyone refuses politely. Finally one brave soul concedes, yes, thank you, he would like a Coke. Then all the rest follow suit. While the party-giver's mother is present, the radio is turned up, there is some group singing, the girls dance together and the boys stand around. Everyone talks, whether dancing or not.

When the mother finally bows out, to go to a movie or to some distant part of the house, the party suddenly changes. Singing and dancing stop, and kissing games hold sway—Post Office, Winks, Spinning the Bottle; these games have many variations and many names. Then comes a midway break, when all the girls troop out to the powder room and the boys talk over the good and bad points, the attractiveness or unattractiveness of each girl. Thereafter, the games may continue, but they are only a prelude to the real business of the evening. This is pairing off into couples. Lights are turned low, and the kissing goes on, no longer as part of a game but couple by couple. In general that is all. The party isn't rough and it breaks up at a reasonable time. One unbreakable rule is that all the food is devoured; there are never any leftovers. Kissing and eats are what these adolescents want. No more, no less. And this is what they generally manage to get at their parties.

In late adolescence, we shall see, parties are different. Kissing games are considered kid stuff, and more "mature" activities take their place.

Sally meets the demands of her school life much as Jimmie

meets them. She has self-confidence and carries out her assignments without undue anxiety. She accepts correction, learns from experience and evaluates both her successes and her failures realistically. Some girls, of course, are not so well-adjusted. Like the boys, they react to school activities according to how well or poorly they passed through the early phases of development, according to whether or not they are fixated in some earlier phase. Since what I have said about boys in this connection can be applied here, I shall cite only one example of school-life problems arising from fixation.

A Calamity Jane is usually found in almost every school group. Like her counterpart described in the previous chapter, she has for some reason retained to too great a degree the characteristics of the late oral phase. Jane is anxious and pessimistic, expecting things to turn out badly—always. She suffers in carrying out each piece of homework, and the fact that her paper is good this week or that she gets an "A" on her examination doesn't help her. She can learn nothing from the experience. Over and over again she anticipates failure.

Sally's out-of-school activities include doing things with boys, games and hikes, swimming and skating, as well as parties. There is, however, a tendency for her to band together with a small group of girls, especially after the onset of menstruation. The group has regular gab fests, while they sew or knit— perhaps aping their mothers. The girls share juicy bits of gossip about their friends, teachers, the neighbors and movie stars in the strictest confidence. And all of it is immediately repeated to other girls, also in the strictest confidence. Much of what they recount is made up out of whole cloth, but so lively are their imaginations that they actually believe their own tall tales. Sally and her friends also like to have "hen" parties, with all boys excluded. These are, in effect, extensions and more formal versions of the group gossip fests. At such a party the girls generally sit in a circle on the floor; they talk and talk, and smoke and smoke.

All that I said in the previous chapter about boys' smoking applies also to girls. The fundamental reasons for wanting to smoke are the same. In addition, girls have a special reason for smoking. It lessens their desire for candy and helps them ward off obesity. The ad man knew this when he wrote, "Reach for a Lucky instead of a sweet"—the slogan that roused the ire of the candy industry.

Like Jimmie, Sally is intensely interested in the movies. Since identification is the basis of her interest, as it is the basis of his, it is to be expected that her tastes are different. Love and romance is what she wants, not adventure stories. Mysteries are tolerated only if they have a love interest. She identifies herself with the movie actresses, and tries to copy their way of dressing, their hairdos, and their way of walking and speaking. She may also "fall in love" with a male movie star and write to him for his autographed picture.

Radio and TV also occupy a great deal of Sally's out-of-school time. Here, too, her tastes are conditioned by identification and thus are different from the tastes of boys. She is rarely interested in sports news and athletic events for themselves alone. She wants to know just enough about the world of sports to be able to discuss it knowingly with her "dates."

Sally does not face the money problem that her brother is up against in this period. Her allowance is usually adequate for her need—ice cream, movies, lunches, carfare and routine cosmetics. If she needs something extra in the way of lipstick, she can generally get supplementary funds from Mother. As for perfume, all she has to do is use Mother's when a heavy date calls for something special. Cigarettes can be taken from the family cache.

If she happens to be going with a boy who cannot afford

to take her to the theater, she can probably persuade her father to provide the tickets, and it is a simple matter to tell her escort a convincing story of how Daddy got stuck with them and now he can't use them. Such subterfuges are not always needed, however, for the practice of going Dutch—she and her young man each paying their own way—is common and common sense in adolescence.

It is no exaggeration to say that clothes are the major interest of adolescent girls. They are avid readers of fashion magazines and the fashion pages of the daily paper. They watch for announcements of sales, and put an enormous amount of thought and time and energy on the problem of being well dressed. Their attitude toward clothes offers clues to their personality development in a clearer way, perhaps than their attitude toward any other single facet of their lives.

Take Doris. When she was a child, her mother loved to dress her "little baby daughter." Now, when she is in her teens, her mother still chooses her clothes and continues to make her look like a little girl, cute and babyish. Doris acquiesces because she is carrying out her mother's wishes, and also because unconsciously this is the way she wants to dress. She is still a baby, still in the oral narcissistic phase of wishing to attract attention, wishing to be petted and made much of. Later on she may substitute overdaring, immodest and inappropriate clothes for the babyish kind. The reason remains the same. She enjoys exhibitionism, wants to attract attention to herself. And this is very different from wanting to be attractive.

Beatrice is the overneat, meticulous kind. No spots, no wrinkles, everything must fit perfectly, everything must be in place. She has more clothes than she can use, for she never discards anything, and she takes such good care of her suits and coats and dresses that they are a long time wearing out. Although she buys dresses that are in style at the time of purchase, she is forever wearing outmoded ones, because she hoards her new things instead of enjoying them. Beatrice is fixated at the anal phase of her development. Her perfectionist traits show up in her clothes.

The well-adjusted girl—the Sally of our story—does not show these extremes of taste and practice. She is interested in clothes, but she uses them as a means, not an end. Her objective is to be attractive. She wants to conform to what is the custom in her crowd—be it strapless dance dresses or blue jeans, and at the same time she wants some individual touches. This is as it should be. Peer culture, as it is called, is especially strong in adolescence when to do as one's peers do gives one added security; and ambivalently, the desire for individual expression is also strong in adolescence, when to do things differently helps to develop a personality of one's own.

Aside from indicating personality traits, the way a young adolescent girl dresses also expresses her special drives. Perhaps she wants to be grown up, far beyond her years. Perhaps she has not put behind her the desire to remain a child. The former is the more general drive. If her slight, budding breasts give her away in her attempts to appear older than she really is, she must stuff out a bra with tissue paper or a handkerchief, or she may take advantage of that new invention, falsies.

One more fact of clothes needs to be touched upon, namely the hostility and antagonism and social withdrawal that so often overwhelm the young girl who must constantly wear the hand-me-downs of an older sister or cousin. Her friends recognize the dresses, which are often hopelessly out of style and unsuited to her figure or looks. Thwarted in her natural desire to be attractive, to choose her own clothes, and be an individual in her own right, this girl feels like the proverbial "poor relation," inferior to her comrades, and unable to compete with them. As a result she may actually withdraw entirely from normal social activities. Rather stay home from the dance than go and have someone whisper that she is wearing her sister's last year's dress and how unbecoming it is on her.

Parents should somehow manage to let a young girl have some things of her own, no matter how inadequate they may be compared with the hand-me-downs. It will cost far less in the end to spend some money on new dresses for a younger daughter, or on yard goods for making them, than to have her personality warped and marred, and pay for costly psychiatric help later on when she is an adult.

I have tried in this chapter to give you a picture of Sally and her girl friends during the first phase of their adolescence— roughly up to about their fifteenth year. As a child Sally was sheltered and protected by her parents. She sought and received from them love and security, reassurance in times of difficulty, guidance and support. During this period of early adolescence her eyes turn away from parents and family. She is beginning to shift for herself, to make her own decisions, and to feel confident of her ability to function in the outside world. Like Jimmie's, her personality is being modified by people and by the happenings in her daily life. She has left behind much of her aggression, her ambivalence has lessened and now focuses largely on accepting or rejecting her role as a woman. This conflict is perhaps not so sharp as it was in former generations, for the adult world today is no longer "a man's world" in which women take a subordinate place. Sally has a far better chance than her mother and grandmother to become a well-adjusted, functioning person who at the same time retains her femaleness.

CHAPTER FOUR

The Adolescent Triangle

IN THE PREVIOUS TWO CHAPTERS I have described Jimmie and Sally in the phase of development called *Early Adolescence*. They now pass into *Middle Adolescence*, so named to differentiate it from the previous period and from the final phase which is the precurser of Adulthood.

In this middle phase, Jimmie and Sally are still ambivalent; and they still have an urgent need to try their powers. Their almost exclusive interest in contemporaries of their own sex has waned. The boy-boy and girl-girl relationships that I have described as typical of early teen-agers are no longer important. There is now an awakening interest in contemporaries of the opposite sex. It is as if the barrier that separates boys and girls is lowered little by little until it melts away.

This shift in focus comes about indirectly, for Jimmie, through a revival of interest in his mother after a temporary turning away from her; and for Sally, similarly, through a revival of interest in her father after a temporary drawing away. It is worth our while to consider these situations in detail, for the way things work out has a profound effect upon the adolescent's future. Whether the foundations of adult life are firm or jerry-built is to a great extent determined by what occurs in this phase of adolescence.

The diagram on this page may help you understand the interplay of forces among the three people chiefly involved in the triangle of adolescence—two males and a female, or two females and a male, as the case may be.

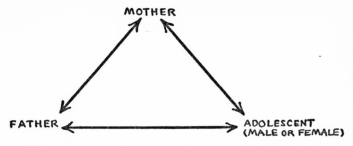

The mother and father, of course, interact upon each other; they have their own relationship as husband and wife, over and above their feelings and reactions as parents. The boy, whose first love as infant and child was his mother, has gone through a period of lessened interest in her as his feelings focused on his father. Now he "finds" her again and at the same time he maintains the relationship he has established with his father. The girl, likewise, "finds" her father again, after a period during which he has been a minor figure in her life, keeping at the same time her close feelings toward her mother. All these reactions are complex and delicately balanced.

Let us see how matters work out for Jimmie. He is beginning to be interested in girls, and he may even have gone through a period of "puppy love." But he is still unsure of himself with contemporaries of the opposite sex. The one woman with whom he feels secure, whose love he need never doubt is his mother. And so his first serious attachment—not as a child to a parent, but as a male to a female—is to his mother, or someone who stands in place of his mother in his life.

Jimmie endows his mother with all the attributes he admires in women. He likes her looks, the color of her hair, or her figure. He is proud of the chocolate cakes and cookies she bakes, the way she runs the household, or the way she does her job if she works outside of the home. He approves of her views and attitudes, and likes all the things that go to make up her personality. Whether or not she is actually good-looking or an excellent cook, or a good saleslady, or an outstanding teacher has little to do with his estimate. His reactions are based on feelings, not on facts. Jimmie wants his mother's love and attention. He wants to hug and kiss her, to talk to her and take her out. She is his "best girl."

If Jimmie's father is wise, he will recognize that this is a temporary phase—and a necessary one—in Jimmie's development. He will recognize that he and Jimmie are "rivals," but only in a surface way and for a short period of time. And so, with tongue in cheek, he helps Jimmie along in his wooing of the female in this domestic triangle. He gives his son some advantages in this game that will soon be played out, so that Jimmie can come through this period with self-confidence and a sense of his own worth.

Perhaps Jimmie has been hoarding his allowance for weeks, and working on Saturday besides, to scrape together the money for that pin or handbag or scarf he wants to buy for his mother's birthday. Perhaps he is in the dumps, knowing he will never make it in time for the Great Day. Dad can slip him a few extra bucks, saying, "This is just between the two of us. Now go on downtown and do your shopping." Another time, Dad can hand his son a pair of theater tickets that have a price tag the young man could never hope to meet, with an offhand, "How about taking your mother to the show? I want a night off for a game of poker." And when his wife makes Jimmie's favorite chocolate cake instead of *his* favorite apple pie, Dad can hide his annoyance, or better still can understand what is going on and not feel slighted.

Each thing the father does is small in itself. Taken together, they add up to an attitude on the father's part that helps to give the young man stability and assurance, and makes it possible for him to take the next step in his development.

It is easy to see what may happen if Jimmie and his Dad actually become rivals for the affection of their "best girl," as two men would in an adult triangle. The father, of course, has an edge on Jimmie if it comes to actual competition for the attention of the woman in the picture. If Jimmie is thwarted in establishing a close loving relationship with his mother, he may have a sense of failure that may make him insecure in his attitudes and actions toward other women later on in life. Similar reactions may result from the mother's failure to understand her son's drive for her affection and love. If she is aloof or actually rebuffs his overtures as "a nuisance," he may feel thwarted and hostile, and this hostility may spread out into hostility toward other women.

Let us assume that both parents understand what is going on and give Jimmie every opportunity to "woo" his mother and play the man's role successfully. It is a role that he will want to play for a relatively short time. Jimmie generally stays attached to his mother—in love with her, one might say—for no more than about two years. During this phase he is beginning to think more like a man and less like a boy. He is noting the relationship between his parents and between other married couples. He is turning to romantic literature, formerly scorned as sissy stuff. Probably he is writing poetry, or at least reading poetry. His interest in girls, already evident in a general way, sharpens under the impetus of his romantic focus on his mother until he singles out some one girl and begins to "go steady" with her.

How does he pick her? Why does he think that Kate is attractive, when she doesn't register at all with his friend Pete? And why does Pete think that Ann is the prettiest of all the girls in the crowd when Jimmie can't see anything in her at all? These matters of taste and attraction are not arbitrary. They follow a definite pattern, but it is a pattern so hidden that most of us are not aware of it.

A boy, obviously, cannot actually be in love with his mother for a protracted period of time, if he is to develop into an adult who can make a normal and satisfactory life for himself. As I have said, normally his period of emotional adolescent attachment to her is comparatively brief. It terminates in his being attracted to a female of his own age who is *like* her—not point for point, but in some noticeable and important ways. Jimmie doesn't know why he likes Kate. She just clicks for him. He may not himself realize that she walks like his mother, with the same springy step, or that she has eyes like his mother's or hair of the same color, or that she moves her hands in the same way when she talks. . . .

I have spoken in previous chapters of *identification* in connection with the adolescent's interest in movies, TV and radio programs, and in connection with Jimmie's attachment to his father or other older man, and Sally's feelings about her mother. The process of identification is at work here, too. Jimmie identifies Kate with his mother, and so he likes her. Pete, whose mother is of course different from Jimmie's mother, does not like Kate, because in his case there is no possibility of identification. The process goes a step further and then still another step. And it goes according to rule, as you will see.

Jimmie, having been attracted to Kate, meets Phyllis and likes her at once. In fact, he likes her more than Kate. Why? She has straight ash blonde hair, not brown wavy hair like his mother's. But she talks like Kate, and tosses her hair back the way Kate does, and perhaps she is awfully keen about people, as Kate is. Never mind that in lots of ways she doesn't resemble Kate at all. Jimmie identifies Phyllis with Kate, and he had liked Kate because he identified her with his mother. Indirectly, as you see, he identifies Phyllis with his mother, although he is probably not aware of it.

During the next few years Jimmie continues to be attracted to one girl after another. His interest shifts by this process of indirect identification, until he finally seriously falls in love.

The old song says, "I want a girl just like the girl that married dear old Dad." But the girl Jimmie chooses may be, and usually is, quite different from his mother in looks, personality, character and accomplishments. She may be short, dark, and vivacious while his mother is tall, blonde, and quiet. She has, nevertheless, been chosen by Jimmie through a process of identification that links her with his mother step by step, as I have described. The important point is that these steps solve, or at least bypass, the problem that would arise if he fell in love with a girl who was in all respects a replica of his mother.

If the young man's wish for a girl "just like" his mother were fulfilled literally, he would have difficulty in making a success of the marriage. You will recall the story of Oedipus, which I touched upon in discussing the Oedipal phase of development. Oedipus unwittingly married his mother, and tragedy and disaster followed in the wake of this unnatural act. He broke the taboo against incest—a taboo that is found in all civilizations and all races. To return to our young man Jimmie, if he married a girl "just like the girl" that married his Dad, he would, psychologically speaking, be breaking the taboo. He would be too much the son, too little the husband, in a marriage with a woman who reminded him too directly and obviously of his mother.

The process of step-by-step identification, of *indirect*

linkage with the mother, makes it possible for a young man to choose a partner who represents his image of the ideal woman —an image that is, of course, based on his ideas of what his mother is like. At the same time the process makes it possible for him to avoid the complications and probable disasters that would arise if he married a girl *just like his mother*.

The girl in this period of Middle Adolescence passes through a phase that is similar to the boy's. She swings back to her father, and he is for a time the one she loves best. This is fine. This is natural and normal, provided that she is not so attached to her father that no man in her own generation appeals to her.

When Sally sets her cap for Daddy, makes a bid for his interest and affection, her mother must be wise and understanding. Just as Jimmie's father, if he is wise, helps his son in his "wooing" of his mother, so Sally's mother will help her. When Sally tries a new hairdo and puts on her most becoming dress to welcome her father on his return from a business trip, Mother will praise her, and throw her husband a hint to admire his daughter and make much of her. Once in a while she will manufacture an excuse to stay home from the movies and let Sally have an evening out alone with her Daddy. Sally's mother will know what to do if she keeps in mind that her daughter is going through a normal phase, and that it will not last long. But if she fails to understand the situation, she may resent playing second fiddle to a younger "female," she may think of Sally as a rival. Then the triangle aspects of the relationship may get out of hand.

If all goes well Sally, like Jimmie, will soon break out of this home triangle formation. She will be drawn to a particular boy because he is like her father. And then she will be attracted to another boy because in some ways he is like the

first boy. The process is the same for girls as for boys. I have
already explained how the choice is made. If matters take
their normal course, Sally is attracted to Bob because, it
seems to her, he is like her father; she is then attracted to Bill
because he is like Bob, although he may be quite different from
her Dad in looks and personality. Step by step, she is getting
farther away from her father's type of man, which is all to
the good. Nevertheless, the man she finally falls in love with
and marries is chosen because of the indirect link with her
first love—her father.

The processes I have described for Sally and Jimmie oper-
ate smoothly when the boy and girl have passed successfully
through the early phases of development, when they have
wise parents who understand what is going on, and are themselves well-adjusted. Matters do not always turn out so fortunately. The difficulties that arise are not the result of fate or
bad luck; if this were the case we could feel pretty pessimistic
about life. They are in large measure created by the parents,
and they can be overcome or at least greatly lessened by the
parents.

At the risk of oversimplifying the situation, I put it this
way: when parents interfere too much, and the natural son-
mother and daughter-father relationships of Middle Adolescence are not allowed to develop, a steppingstone to adulthood is missing. The adolescent may be incapable, then, of
transferring the love for the parent of the opposite sex to a
contemporary. As we have seen, this transfer is essential for
advancing into the next phase of development.

The boy cannot have a close relationship with his mother
if his father is jealous; the father is obviously the stronger
and more successful rival in a contest between father and son.
Thwarted in obtaining love satisfaction from the mother, the

boy may be unable to make a relationship with girls. He may, as a result, be unable to find a mate and may remain a "middle adolescent," or even regress to an "early adolescent," whatever his actual age. Likewise, the girl, outmaneuvered by a mother who is jealous of the mutual interest and love of father and daughter, may stay in this phase of adolescence and never achieve a successful relationship with a man of her own generation.

It should not be too difficult for parents to understand these processes—and to act accordingly.

Parents, however, are themselves "people" with their own difficulties. It is simple for me to say that your children will fare best if you are well-adjusted and unfixated. It is far from simple, I know, to attain this goal. As a psychiatrist I am keenly aware that each person has his individual problems and that few of us have passed through our own development unscathed. In a later chapter I shall discuss some situations that are outgrowths of the parents' personality difficulties. For the present, we are concerned with what may be called normal personalities and normal home situations.

Boys and girls in the period of middle adolescence, I noted earlier in this chapter, have a growing awareness of the quality of the relationship between their parents and between other couples with whom they are in close contact. Edging forward to the time when they themselves will choose mates and embark upon matrimony, they watch their elders with critical and often disapproving eyes. Their ideas about marriage are based on what they see. There are many reasons why every couple should work toward developing a good marriage. One of the most cogent ones for parents is that the quality of their marriage—be it "good" or "bad"—has a profound effect on their children, and especially on their adolescent son and daughter.

Jimmie and Sally—the young people of our story—are nearing the end of their journey through childhood and adolescence. The choice of a mate and the making of a marriage relationship are still in the future. Nevertheless, it is fitting to discuss the meaning of love and marriage here, for our young people have a greater chance of achieving a satisfactory marriage if this is the kind that their parents have achieved, the kind they see in their own homes as adolescents.

In defining a wholesome and emotionally sound marriage, I often say that it is based on three Cs—*Communication, Consideration* and *Co-operation.* Husband and wife are able to communicate with each other in the fullest sense of the term, to express any and all of their thoughts to each other with confidence that they will be understood. They are considerate of one another. This quality of consideration, since it is rooted in identification, gives to each of them something beyond the boundaries of self. When husband and wife see life through each other's eyes, their horizons widen, and they gain a greater understanding of life than either could have alone. Finally, there is mutual co-operation, the strong urge, translated into action, to be mutually helpful. When a marriage has these three elements, it will develop ever deeper meaning and ever more rewarding experiences.

Genuine love, on which a secure marriage is based, is a desire to be close to another person, to wish fervently for that person's happiness. It begins with a feeling of one's own inferiority, helplessness and dependence. The loved one, it is felt, is stronger, more competent, and more admirable, and can make up for one's own lacks and inadequacies. Husband and wife each have these feelings. Soon, through identification, each takes on some of the attributes with which the partner has been endowed. Thus they interact upon one another, they grow together and develop together.

Freud, who made basic contributions to psychiatry, defined the state of being in love as "a group of two." A group, he said, is more than a collection of people. Like an individual, it has a personality, which is more than and different from the sum of the personalities of the individuals of which it is composed. It has an emotional core, as an individual has, that enables it to function as a unit. If that emotional core has integrity, the group will be able to meet challenging situations with a sense of satisfaction. In applying this concept of a group to the state of being in love, Freud was saying that two people who are genuinely in love are a unit, with a special and unique personality that is more potent than the personalities of the two partners added together.

A true marriage is a group in this sense of the term. It is, I think, the strongest and most beneficial relationship that human beings have developed. It is a force for good—for the husband and wife, for their children, and for all other persons with whom they come in contact.

CHAPTER FIVE

On the Threshold of Adulthood

Late Adolescence

WE HAVE FOLLOWED Jimmie and Sally on their journey through infancy and childhood and the first two phases of adolescence. They now start on the final stretch of the road that leads to adulthood, which is called, for convenience, *Late Adolescence*. What are Jimmie and Sally like at this time?

I have already touched upon the increasing importance of the environment, as Jimmie and Sally grow and develop, and the ever greater effect of outside forces upon their personalities. By the time late adolescence is reached, identification with parents—copying their attitudes and actions, taking the home ideas into the outside world—has waned. Our young people are beginning to feel independent of the all-powerful, all-pervading father and mother figures. Their relationship with their parents now has fewer elements of conflict, and as a result it is on a more even keel than in the foregoing years.

Day-by-day situations are no longer handled primarily on the basis of home viewpoints and identification with parents. Contact with contemporaries and with teachers, neighbors and other adults has given Jimmie and Sally another basis for their attitudes and actions. This different approach is strengthened by their greater capacity for independent thinking, as they develop mentally.

Thus Jimmie and Sally are better able to understand other people and how they function. They can differentiate between desires that are attainable and those beyond their reach. The former they try to fulfill through their own deliberations and their own efforts; the latter, they are now able to label in their minds as aspirations. Because they can thus differentiate, they no longer need to take refuge in the daydreaming that characterizes the earlier phases of adolescence. They can make compromises when necessary, and postpone a satisfaction that cannot be gained immediately.

Our young people are slowly gaining mastery over themselves. They are learning how to avoid painful situations and how to reassure themselves when such situations must be faced. In sum, they have more confidence in their ability to stand on their own feet, and the conflict of desires for independence and protection has to a large extent been resolved.

Jim—he has by now outgrown his childhood name—is working toward a man-to-man relationship with his father. He no longer thinks of Dad as an enemy, and he is antagonistic and irritated only when Dad refuses to listen to him or discuss matters that seem important to him. He assumes some responsibility for his mother's happiness and is generally kindly disposed toward her. Yet, because he is moving away from her emotionally, he is sometimes irked by the mother-son ties that he does not know how to break.

As for Sally, her interest in boys and men of her own generation have changed her attitude toward her father. She no longer needs to make a bid for his admiration or tries to impress him with her female attractiveness. She mothers him a little bit, listens to him in a somewhat condescending way, but she is not very much involved with him. By the same token, Sally's animosity toward her mother as a rival for Daddy's affection is dying out. She begins to have interests in common with Mother, even a sort of older sister feeling. She wants to help Mother buy her clothes and change her hairdo for something more becoming. Thus the tables are turned, with Sally taking the lead in feminine concerns, instead of being led.

This is, of course, the ideal picture. Life does not usually conform so neatly to a pattern or arrange itself so simply. Parents find it hard to relinquish the job that has filled their lives during all the years of child-raising. Women, especially, are loath to stop "mothering" their growing children—these boys and girls who are soon to be men and women. Parents are often not themselves mature enough to let their youngsters shift their interests from the home to the outside world and to people of their own age. This is perhaps the most difficult period for the parents of adolescents. The time of storm and stress is almost over. That very fact brings home to parents the realization that the job of rearing their children is nearly finished, and that other activities must take its place.

I have pointed out that Jim and Sally no longer have the ambivalence that is rooted in conflict about adult versus childhood roles. Now, however, they have a different kind of ambivalence, born of conflict within themselves. At this age many momentous decisions must be made. Chief among them are decisions about jobs and education, and about sex and family relationships. The young people fear the consequences of whatever course of action they decide upon, and yet they *must* (they feel) make their *own* decisions. They are anxious and tense about many things—problems of emancipation from the home setup; problems about themselves, their looks, their physical skills, their intellectual capacities; problems about education, jobs and sex.

Many of their worries may not be based on facts or on past experience. Jim may have come through high school at the head of his class, but this does not keep him from worrying about whether he will flunk out during his freshman year at college. Sally may likewise worry about marks, or she may be sick with fright about how things will go at her first college prom despite ample proof in the past of her attractiveness. It is as if anxiety were part of the pattern of this period. Considering how many problems confront these young people—how many matters must, somehow, be decided at this time—it is not surprising that they are tense and disturbed, ambivalent in an inner sense.

Foremost in the minds of adolescents in this period is the choice of a vocation or job. Many forces are at work in helping or hindering them as they try to make this choice. Personality make-up is perhaps the predominant factor. Other elements that enter into the choice are mental endowment, economic opportunity, parental attitudes and the intricate processes of wanting to follow in the footsteps of some adult—or of vehemently not wanting to do so.

Let us go back for a moment to the phases of development during infancy and childhood in considering personality traits. Certain characteristics, you will recall, are normal and natural in each of these phases. Each one of us retains *some* of the characteristics of every phase through which we pass, and generally retains *more* characteristics of some one phase than of the others. I am not speaking here of fixation—the undue, disproportionate retention of the attributes of the oral phase, for example, or of some other phase—but of the normal process. What we retain to a large extent determines our personality, our aptitudes and liking for certain types of work. The individual will probably function best in an occupation in which the specific characteristics that are predominant in him are most useful.

Betty, let us say, has more characteristics from the oral phase than from other phases. These traits may be exceedingly useful to her if she chooses to be an actress, a model, or a salesgirl. They might, on the other hand, make her dissatisfied with a job as laboratory technician or librarian. Sam, in whom oral characteristics also predominate, very likely will do well as a salesman or public speaker. Individuals with characteristics of the late anal phase will probably make good as builders, dentists, surgeons, technicians and efficiency workers. The characteristics of the phallic phase are useful for the businessman, the promoter, the entrepeneur.

Put in this way, the entire matter of vocational aptitudes is, of course, oversimplified, with the distortions that inevitably accompany attempts at simplifying complex ideas and processes.

Theoretically, the most eminent artists, scientists, statesmen, and so on, somehow have the capacity for merging and unifying all the characteristics of the various phases of their development. They have personalities that are balanced and integrated, that are wide-ranging. They are richly endowed and are able to succeed, in the true sense of the word, in almost any field.

Most of us are not so fortunate. We must make the most of what we have. A number of tests are in use today, however, which can assist adolescents (and their parents) in understanding their natural capacities. With such tests a young man would not set his heart on being a surgeon or a dentist, for example, only to learn too late that he lacked the necessary manual dexterity for such a profession, however well-endowed he was in other respects.

These personality characteristics are not, of course, the only elements that enter into the choice of a vocation. There are varying degrees of mental capacity. Put it bluntly, some people have better minds than others. There is the cold hard fact of economic opportunity, of how far a family can go in financing its children's education. Aside from money, parents have different attitudes toward education.

"Now it's time to get down to work," one father says when his son graduates from high school. "I didn't have it so easy—went to work for two bucks a week when I was fourteen. So cut out this nonsense about college and engineering, and get yourself a job."

In another family, with no more money and no more educational background, the father says, "I don't want you to stop now and get into a blind alley job, son. I want you to have more of a chance than your old man had. Mom and I think you should make a try at college. We've saved enough for your first year, and after that maybe you can manage for yourself."

Sometimes the choice of a vocation is based on what father does, or ironically enough on what father does *not* do. A lad who feels strong enough to become a better doctor, for example, than his old man, who is a doctor, may well choose a medical career just because he wants to compete with his father and win out. On the other hand, if he has always been shown up as inferior to his father, he may eliminate competition by not wanting to become a doctor and by choosing some totally unrelated profession or occupation.

The choice may be made on the basis of admiration for some other adult—a teacher, close relative or neighbor. The danger of a choice made solely on such a basis, and also solely on the basis of the father-son (or daughter) relationship, is that it fails to take into account many other factors that should be considered. Foremost among these are personal traits and the aptitudes that come from them, as I have tried to show. The point is illustrated in the following story of one of my patients.

Ted's family lived on what we call "the wrong side of the tracks" in a smallish town. His father had a steady job as a drugstore clerk, there were two younger brothers and a sister, and life was pretty dull. On the ground floor of the two-family house in which Ted's family lived, was a doctor with a busy practice. Ted throughout his childhood watched the comings and goings, the hasty ringing of the doctor's bell in the dead of night, the doctor dashing out with his little black satchel, the people who crowded his waiting room day after day. This was exciting. This was the way to be important, to have people at your beck and call. And the doctor became Ted's hero. When he grew up, he would be a doctor, too.

No thought was given to aptitudes or finances, only to making this fixed childhood idea come true. It was only after heartbreaking struggle and frustrating years at medical school that an older and a wiser Ted realized that he was totally unsuited in temperament to be a doctor. It was only after disappointment and inner conflict brought him to me as a patient that he found out about his aptitudes and natural endowments. Today Ted is a successful actor. He is important and sought after, his life is exciting. His dream has come true, but on a more realistic basis than a child's hero worship for the doctor downstairs.

To sum up—the adolescent should make his own choice of a vocation. He should be helped to make it wisely, but his parents should never—I repeat, never—coerce him into a decision. If Mr. B. has a thriving garage and wants his son Jack to step into the business, well and good if that is what Jack wants. But if he doesn't like machinery, doesn't like to get his hands dirty and crawl around under a car, then don't force him into the business, however good it might be for him financially. Sometimes coercion works negatively. Sidney's father was a piano teacher in a small town. He was fairly good, but not spectacular, and he had a hard time earning enough to take care of his family. No son of his, he vowed, was going to be a musician. So Sidney pleaded in vain for music lessons. Put into an uncle's grocery business, he was a conspicuous failure. Long years afterwards, he broke out of this arbitrary pattern set up by his father to "protect" him, and became a trumpet player in a dance band. What he might have achieved, given encouragement and opportunity to develop his natural bent, no one, of course, can say.

Professional assistance can be obtained in finding out what young boys and girls are suited for. Skilled vocational counselors can help. Many high schools now have such people as regular members of their staffs. Aptitude tests reveal much. Sometimes a few talks with a psychiatrist will clarify things and give definite focus to the young person's vague aspirations.

Many young people, of course, go to college before they face the necessity for choosing a vocation. In former times, a generation and more ago, it was chiefly the specially gifted or the specially fortunate economically who went on to higher education after high school. Today college is the accepted pattern for a large number of our young people.

How well Jim and Sally get along at college depends upon the foundations of character built during their formative years. Sometimes going to college does not mean leaving home, but in the main it is synonymous with a break away from family life and calls for adjustment to a quite different way of living. Fraternities and sororities in the recent past came in for much criticism because of their undemocratic practices, and because they excluded too many young people from their bonds of fellowship. Today there is less ground for such criticism. These groups serve a definite purpose in that they are substitute *families* for the boys and girls not yet ready for living without any family. There are older and younger siblings, with the familiar patterns of bossing and being bossed, even as at home; there is "family" solidarity and loyalty. Thus fraternities and sororities in a sense help the college boy and girl in their adjustment to living away from home.

Jim and Sally and their friends go to college for a variety of reasons. Some, consciously or unconsciously, want to postpone the time when serious choices in life must be made. Some want the prestige of being "college-bred" and they get by with as little work as possible and as much loafing as possible —with ample opportunity to satisfy their desire to play. Some want to bolster their egos by eminence in athletics, club activities, class leadership and the like. And some, of course, are activated by a genuine desire for learning and scholastic achievement.

Whatever the underlying motivation, college has a profound effect on the adolescent. He makes new friends, learns to function independently, and—let it be hoped—widens the horizons of his mind.

Aside from the all-important business of choosing a vocation, Jim and Sally are finding themselves socially. There is a great need for independence on the threshold of adulthood. Jim wants to prove to himself and the world that he is a man. Sally's focus is somewhat different. She is already thinking in terms of marriage and for this she too must try her wings.

Jim should have his own latchkey. There should be no questions about where he is going, and no arguments about what time he comes home. For better or for worse, he must now look after himself. If you insist that he must be home and in bed by midnight, you will surely drive him into lying and deceit. It's true, as you may say to him, that there's nothing he can or should do after midnight that he cannot do before that hour. But this is not a matter of logic. Jim just has to assert his manhood, and one of the symbols of that manhood—that laying aside the years of childhood—is to come home at whatever hour suits him.

In all likelihood he's doing nothing wrong—and if he is, you can't stop him at this stage by coercion. His activities, necessary for him at this age, are bull sessions, dances, sitting around in beer joints, riding to and fro in his dad's or some other dad's car, being the life of some party.

Sally, too, must have leeway. If you put a curfew on when she must be home from a dance or party, she will feel that you don't trust her, and may well live up to your idea of how she behaves. Incidentally, her young man will look around for some less strictly brought up girl, and she won't thank you for "interfering."

Adults never cease being amazed at the physical energy of adolescents in their upper teens. Dancing, swimming, tennis, hikes, night school if they are at work, clubs for pleasure and self-improvement—the list is almost endless. To take some liberty with the poet's words, in the bright lexicon of youth there is no such word as tired.

Dancing is perhaps the most popular activity of boys and girls in the late adolescent period. It provides intimate contact between the sexes and an opportunity to exert and respond to sex attraction. It also fulfills practically all the essentials of play at this age. Dancing is purposeful in a mild way and is therefore "fun" without being boring. It enhances the ego, in that it calls for personal grace, some skill, suitable dress and social etiquette. The rhythm and the opportunity to express the feelings aroused by the music provide added pleasure.

We often forget that modern social dancing is only one form of this age-old activity, and that long before Christianity dancing had religious ceremonial significance. Girls are usually interested in dancing at an earlier age than boys, but there is a rising liking for this activity as adolescence progresses. By late adolescence, both boys and girls, in conscious anticipation of marriage, want to meet and get to know many persons of the opposite sex in order to test out their congeniality. Dancing seems to be the ideal medium for satisfying this desire.

In a previous chapter I described the typical parties of early adolescence. The difference between these parties and those of late adolescence show clearly the difference between the two phases. The typical party to which Jim and Sally go as late adolescents is, like the earlier ones, generally given by one of the girls in the group. It also consists of about six boys and six girls. Now, however, the guests come as couples, instead of all arriving together for mutual reassurance. Each boy has his special girl. Kissing games are ruled out as kid stuff, and there are no awkward preliminaries of group singing and fooling with the radio or TV. Dancing is the order of the evening, and the participants plunge into it at once. The furniture is pushed to the walls, the rug is rolled back, the lights are dimmed, and the couples dance—generally cheek to cheek. The voracious appetite of early adolescence, that made all the food at parties disappear as if by magic, has changed to nibbling. Food is not important, and there is no serious drinking.

Nevertheless, drinking is a problem at this age, and one that gives parents much concern, especially the parents of adolescent boys. Although there is no taboo today against "nice girls" drinking, they do not as a rule drink to the extent of creating a problem, as do some boys. I discussed in an earlier chapter the forces that make adolescents want to smoke. Drinking likewise satisfies basic needs. Alcohol diminishes inhibitions, it heightens self-esteem and temporarily keeps anxiety at bay. Obstacles appear less insurmountable, undesirable conflicts can be put out of mind. Some adolescent boys also drink to obtain oral gratification, to get even with Mother—unconsciously, of course. It is as if the boy says, or rather feels, I didn't get enough to drink from you as an infant; now I'll *take* as much as I want. On a more conscious level, adolescents in this late period drink because they want to do what adults do, and because they want to go along with their crowd—do what their peers do.

The problem of drinking cannot be solved by prohibitions and rules. It will do no good to forbid it, any more than it will do any good to forbid smoking. The best advice I can give you as parents is to set a good example of moderate socially acceptable drinking, in the hope that your son will stay within the limits you set for yourself. Above all, do not make drinking forbidden fruit. If you and your friends have a drink before dinner, offer Jim one too, as a matter of course. Likewise, if you have wine at the table, Jim's glass should be filled along with those of the grownups. In other words, satisfy his urgent need to be an adult, and also set him the example of how one can drink without becoming a slave to a vice.

Physiologically, one or two drinks a day after thirty years of age is probably beneficial, in that alcohol stimulates circulation. In this respect, the time tables, as it were, for drinking and smoking are in direct reverse. Smoking, our mores to the contrary, has few detrimental effects in youth, but constricts circulation in adulthood, as I have already pointed out. Alcohol, inasmuch as it warps judgment and is difficult to use in moderation, should—in theory—be avoided in youth or kept at a minimum, but can be beneficial in adulthood.

One reason why adolescent drinking is so serious a problem is that the combination of drinking and driving spells danger and tragedy. It is the rare adolescent who abides by the

slogan—"If you drink, don't drive; if you drive, don't drink."
To get in a car and go places gives the adolescent in his late
teens a sense of power, a feeling of mobility and independence.
The family car will do, but his urgent desire is to have a car of
his own. The "hot rods" that are a menace on the roads are
driven by boys whose urge for power and adventure is so
great that the ordinary car, fast as it is, does not satisfy them.
These boys show the characteristics of the oral phase—they
are carefree, irresponsible, and omnipotent, and in addition
there is an element of masochism. The dangers of driving a hot
rod at top speed are denied, they are assuaged as though by
magic. They can control the gods, nothing can happen to
them—yet some of them are killed and maimed for life. These
lads have a masochistic component in their personality make-up
that demands satisfaction.

Girls usually do not have this urgent need for driving fast
and far, just as they do not have so urgent a need for drinking.
You will recall that in the chapters on early adolescence I
made the point that boys' childhood traits persist, that "boys
and men will be boys," but that girls drop their childhood
traits and tend to become women. These differences in development serve to explain why the urge for fast and dangerous
driving and for drinking are not identical. In almost all other
pursuits, however—tennis, swimming, games of all kinds—girls'
tastes are the same as boys'. Card games and chess are popular.
These activities permit the young people to prove their ade-
quacy to themselves, and to exercise their skill. However,
they often have a notion that, regardless of their ability, they
need luck in order to win. "Luck" does not enter into the
picture, and they should never depend upon it.

In view of the lurid exposés of so-called high school im-
morality, it may sound strange to say that in general boys
and girls in late adolescence are not eager for sexual inter-

course. Jim may have had this experience with a compliant girl or a prostitute, in order to boast of his exploits and parade before his cronies as a he-man, but he is usually disappointed because in his romantic imaginings he had anticipated something quite different. His actual sex experience, carried out furtively, explodes his romantic phantasy; it does not—he finds—miraculously transform him into a grown-up man. Instead, it leaves him dissatisfied and full of guilt and anxiety. What Jim wants is love. Sometimes he learns the hard way that sex and love are not synonymous, but that sex is a by-product of love.

Above all, at this time, Jim wants a girl who will be his confidante, his comrade, ever ready to listen with interest to what he has to say, ever ready to sympathize with him, to understand him. He also wants to "pet" with his girl, to fondle her, rest his head on her breast, kiss her nipples. He may go further, and want his girl to masturbate him, but there he generally stops.

Sally, too, wants a close relationship with her special boy friend. She talks endlessly with him on the telephone, and woe to any member of the family who listens in. But preferably, she and her young man spend long hours talking together and petting, sitting cheek to cheek, holding hands, and experimenting with long smothering kisses. Sally not only takes on the role that her young man wants her to play, she also has a great need to conform to what her peers do, and to her peers this is the accepted way in which to act.

Both boys and girls during this period are primarily immersed in the business of heterosexual adjustment. They are not yet ready for the final consummation of sexual intercourse. Through their petting they are developing feelings for the opposite sex and genuine affection for their partners. They are bolstering their own egos, basking in admiration and approval given and taken. "Making love," in the way that young boys and girls make love, is an incentive for further development.

You will recall that Sally in early adolescence was preoccupied with clothes and fashions. This interest persists. Its basis is that she wants to be as attractive as "the other girls." She tries to look just like whoever is currently the most attractive young woman of stage or screen, and she generally succeeds. Jim, too, continues his interest in clothes, but his motive is to be attractive to his special girl rather than to be like some movie star. And the current fashion among his peers is what forms his taste and his choice of clothes.

All these interests and drives and activities add up to a desire for independence, to a final breakaway from parental domination and protection, as the late adolescent approaches the goal of adulthood. Almost invariably, his attitude toward religion—whatever the sect in which he has been reared— follows this pattern.

I spoke in an earlier chapter about the beginnings of religious beliefs and concepts. Young children feel that their parents are always with them, cherishing them and enveloping them with never-failing love and protection. When, in any one of a number of ways, they first become aware of death, they quickly translate this knowledge into a realization that their parents, too, will die. They turn, unconsciously to the concept of God as the Supreme Father, who can never forsake them. God as the Father figure is the basis of all religions, however they may differ in dogma and rituals of worship.

During early adolescence religion is taken pretty much for granted. The young boy and girl follow the family pattern in attending services, going to Sunday School, accepting the ceremonies of confirmation. All these activities suggest the comforting nearness of God and also the desire to stay close to the parents by doing as they do, believing as they believe.

Then comes a change. On the threshold of adulthood there is, as I have tried to show in this chapter, a great unconscious desire for emancipation, for breaking away from the father's domination. In so doing, there is also a desire to break away from the domination of the Supreme Father. The late adolescent generally goes through a period of religious doubt. He withdraws from formal religious practices, rebels against what seems to him to be the authoritarian attitude of the leaders of his church. He wants to rely on his *own* moral code, not on some code that he is told to obey. His code, of course, has been inculcated in him during all the years of his development, it is not something he has suddenly thought out for himself even though he may believe that this is so.

The college student's squawks at attending chapel services, however happily he went to church in his earlier years, is a well-known sign of this late adolescent revolt against accepted religious practices. The long bull sessions about religious dogma and the Bible, the questioning of hitherto unquestioned ideas are also signs.

When our young men and women have finally crossed over into adulthood, they will no longer have the adolescent's great need to be free of all shackles, divine as well as human. No longer threatened by their own fathers but on an equal footing with them, they will not feel impelled to deny or reject the Supreme Father. They will in all likelihood reestablish their relationship with their God and live by the ethical precepts of their chosen creed; or they may refrain

from aligning themselves with any creed and yet live according to an ethical code. In either case, they no longer rebel
blindly against divine or ethical authority. They are religious
in the broad and true meaning of the word.

PART TWO

Problems and Pitfalls
of Adolescence

In the foregoing chapters, I have described the normal processes of development from infancy to the threshold of adulthood by telling the story of Jimmie and Sally. What happens to these young persons is what usually happens if all goes well and development proceeds in a normal way. Sometimes things do not work out so well. Problems arise that must be faced and if possible solved; pitfalls yawn that must be recognized and if possible avoided. The following chapters discuss these matters.

We must leave Jimmie and Sally, happily arrived at the threshold of adulthood, and consider some of their less fortunate contemporaries who for one or another reason have not made so safe and direct a journey. It is my earnest wish that the material should not disturb or alarm you. Rather, that it should help you and your adolescent sons and daughters recognize certain situations that present difficulties. Knowledge and understanding are the weapons with which we can attack and conquer difficulties. The following chapters seek to provide you with these weapons.

CHAPTER SIX

Adjustment to the Physical Self

JOHNNY HAD WANTED A DOG for many months. He had saved dimes and quarters from his allowance, and had carefully put by what he earned for household chores. Finally the great day arrived when he had ten dollars—the price of a puppy at the nearby kennel—and he went proudly to pick out "his dog." The handsome spaniel had a litter of five. Four of them were saucy, robust little creatures, tumbling about and enjoying life; the fifth was timid and frightened. Something was wrong with its left forepaw and it limped.

"I'll take that one," Johnny said, pointing to the little weakling and ignoring the four robust pups.

"You're making a mistake, son," the kennelman said gravely. "I don't like to let you buy that fellow. Something's the matter with him. Better take one of the others."

"I know something's the matter with him," Johnny replied. Then he pulled up his dungarees and exposed a brace on his left leg. "Something's the matter with me, too. That dog's going to need a lot of understanding and I know how to give it to him. I don't care if he limps. I limp too."

Certain of his choice, Johnny picked up the little weakling, paid his ten dollars and took his dog home.

Johnny had had polio as a child of four. He had made a good recovery, but he did wear a brace and he did limp. He had himself needed a lot of understanding, and quite obviously he had received it from his parents. As a result he didn't recoil from a crippled forepaw or a crippled leg. He didn't have to pretend that he was perfectly strong and sound. In other words, he had adjusted to his handicap. It was there, but it didn't matter.

If parents are overprotective of the child who has been made infirm by polio, if they try to compensate for his "misfortune" by giving him whatever he demands and doing his bidding at every turn, they keep him in the oral (infant) phase of his development. Normally, as I have explained earlier in this book, he would have passed through this phase and into another and still another. Instead, because they indulge him, he continues to feel omnipotent, he monopolizes the environment and is selfish and inconsiderate, just as a baby is. He gets emotionally upset when he doesn't get his way, just as a baby does. These traits very likely will stay with him throughout his life.

Parents should accept the child as he is. They should not deny his physical handicap or defect. They should let the child function, within the limits of his physical capacity, just as a physically normal child functions, and they should treat him just as they would treat any child.

What happens when they do this? Johnny, who limps and wears a brace, will not be caught at the infant stage of development. He will progress normally and successfully through childhood and adolescence. Granted that he cannot play football, cannot take all-day hikes, or go out for the hockey team. Instead of dwelling unhappily on the things he cannot do, he will focus on the things he *can* do. As the song goes, he will "accentuate the positive. . . ." Doubtless he will be able to excel in many ways—perhaps become the president of his class, or win a place on the debating team, or manage some athletic event or dramatic performance. He will belong to the group on a par with his peers and win their admiration.

Matters are not so simple if polio strikes in adolescence instead of childhood. Then the young person may have what seems to be an irrational sense of guilt about the misfortune that has overtaken him. It is not really irrational if we remember that the adolescent hovers from extremes of laxity to extremes of self-righteousness. Social drinking and card playing by the adults around him may be magnified in his mind into "orgies," and he may feel that he or his parents are "wicked" when there is nothing to warrant such conclusions.

Joe, who was a husky lad, got polio in his mid-teens. He felt that he was being punished for something—perhaps for some irregular behavior of his parents. He blamed his parents for what had happened to him. He felt that God was trying to show them the error of their ways by punishing him. So, all his troubles were their fault. This chain of "reasoning" started from hostility toward his parents and led to ever more hostility. It was only a step then to hostility toward the outside world.

The solution of this problem of polio in adolescence is also love and understanding. If the relationship between the boy and his parents is a good one, then both he and they can accept any handicap that he may have, however much it may change his life, and can surmount it.

I have opened this chapter with a discussion of polio because this illness is so much in the public eye and the physical handicaps that sometimes accompany it are definite and readily discernible. There are many other physical conditions or defects that create problems in adolescence. Some of them are temporary, and some are amenable to correction, as we shall see. Some—like Johnny's limp—must be lived with and adjusted to.

Whatever the physical defect or deviation from the accepted "normal," its effect on the adolescent's personality is determined by the attitude of the adolescent himself, the attitude of his peers and the attitude of his parents. The effect of all these attitudes is clearly shown in the various reactions to what are considered deviations in height and weight. When adolescents are thought to be too short or too tall, too fat or too thin—it matters little whether the estimate is made by themselves, their comrades or their parents—there is much uneasiness and unhappiness. Sometimes these attitudes have serious and lasting effects on the personality.

Increases in weight and height from birth to adulthood take place in cycles in which a general pattern may be seen. During the first five years, there is a great gain in height and a proportionately smaller gain in weight. Thereafter, for some six years or so, the process is reversed, and from twelve or thirteen years of age until full growth is attained height again takes the lead. We have, in our society, general ideas about what is a normal height for men and women, and when people deviate greatly from this norm we are apt to say they are "too short" or "too tall."

One could answer with a wisecrack and say, "too short for *what?*" In some countries, where the men are short, five feet five inches seems like a good stature for a man, but in countries where the average height is six feet and over, a man of this size appears to be stunted. All that the "too" means is that the person is noticeably different from the average.

Pete was a shorty. He stopped growing at fifteen instead of continuing to shoot up like most of his comrades. All his daydreams were about himself as a tall strong hero, capable of daring and heroic deeds. And all these wishes, which occupied him to such an extent that he became almost a hermit, were reinforced by his parents' attitude.

"Well, we're not really worried," his Dad says to a neighbor within his son's earshot. "Pete will surely put on a few more inches before he's done growing. It's a handicap for a chap to be small, of course. I hope he makes it." No reassurance here. No help for Pete in accepting himself as he is.

Pete probably appears to be much younger than he is, for we tend, somewhat illogically, to equate short with young and tall with grown-up. His parents, in effect, reject him as a young man and treat him as a child. They probably make few or no physical demands on him and ask for his help only for minor household chores. No one expects Pete to cut down a tree or lever a rock into a better position in the garden. He is pressed into service only to sweep the porch, help dry the dishes, and possibly wash the windows.

Because he looks young and seems weak, and perhaps effeminate, Pete isn't popular with girls of his own age, and thus he misses out on the boy-girl contacts he should normally be having. As for boys, they don't want to pal around with a kid, and he's certainly not sought after for the basketball, baseball or track team. So, if he goes with boys at all, they are younger ones, who are more like him in height than boys of his own age. He continues to be occupied with childish activities and to have childish attitudes long after the time for them is over.

The bantam may try ruses to make himself taller. He may put pads of paper in his shoes or spend his savings for mysterious apparatus that will "stretch his joints." Only after tragic disappointments will he learn that a man by taking thought cannot add a cubit to his height. He may try the opposite approach, preen himself on his superior intelligence and lord it over the big "dumb" boys. He may swagger around with overbearing conceit and become a "little Caesar."

Often, little sawed-off is made a mascot of the gang. He is the one who is made to climb through the transoms and half-opened windows when the boys want to break into a locked classroom or, more seriously, a locked house or store. He may be forced to do whatever some taller, stronger boy wants him to do, and he may "buy" peace and a tenuous friendship by stealing money at home to stand treat to this one boy or the whole crowd.

The short boy is inconspicuous at school and unnoticed in a group. In both situations he has a sense of not belonging. The easy way out is to withdraw, to take refuge in phantasy. Like Walter Mitty, Pete creates a private life for himself to compensate for what he misses in actual life.

The point I want to drive home is that he would not *have* to miss out. His reactions are the result of the attitudes of his parents, his peers and himself toward his height.

I have described the "too short" adolescent boy in detail because the effect of his so-called deviation from what is considered normal height may be taken as a pattern for the effect of other deviations in height—in both boys and girls.

Jennie, if she is small, has much the same difficulties as Pete. Her parents may worry about her. Girls of her own age may give her the cold shoulder and force her to go around with younger girls. But her chief difficulty is her own attitude. This is because parents and peers disapprove less of Jennie because she is "undersized" than they do of Pete. In our society we do not seem to think that girls, like boys, should ideally be tall, and hence it is not a misfortune if they are short.

So Jennie may accept and like being petite and make the most of it. She may, however, try to remain a child in actions since she looks so much like a child. We all know kittenish, babyish young girls and women who dress like children of ten and try perpetually to be "cute." Sometimes such actions come from the fact that they are as short as the child of ten and feel that they must play a corresponding role. Jennie may, like Pete, live in a phantasy world in which she is tall and looks like a modern Juno. I recall a small and really quite pretty girl in high school. The boys were eager to take her out, to dance with her, but she would have none of it. She was somehow unable to see that she was good looking and had a nice figure; she could only see that she didn't measure up to a preconceived notion of what she wanted to be. "Next time I'm born," she would say, "I'm going to be tall and thin and wear long green velvet dresses with trains." None of the boys thought that was attractive, but she clung to her dream instead of accepting and liking reality.

Similar forces are at work, in reverse, in the over-tall lad and the tall gal. The tall boy is idealized. He is often the teacher's favorite and is popular with the girls. Adults are apt to think he is some years older than he actually is, and he is constantly getting into situations with which he cannot cope. Treated as an adult before he is ready for this role, he is likely to be anxious, embarrassed and confused. Sometimes he defends himself against such situations by stubborn resistance to social demands. Because he is able to control younger and smaller boys he may overestimate his worth with his so-called inferiors, as a cover-up of his feeling of inferiority with adults.

The over-tall girl seems to be pushed by invisible hands into a grown-up role. She attempts to justify her height by pretending to be older than she is. Like the over-tall boy, she gets into tight spots because she is trying to play a role, and is asked to play a role, for which she is not ready. She is probably awkward in sports and avoids them to keep from making a spectacle of herself. Because she towers above most of her partners at a dance she dislikes dancing, and she attempts to minimize her height and avoid being conspicuous by hunching her shoulders, stooping, and lowering her head—the debutante slouch. She is not ready, psychologically, to live up to her height, to envisage it as an asset instead of a liability. The line of least resistance is to withdraw from the normal social life of her age group and to become solitary and morose.

Somehow these young boys and girls must learn that there is no "best" height; that it is just as good to be short as tall, and tall as short. They must live with themselves as they are. This they can do only if their parents have the right attitude and understand how to help them.

Despite this plea for acceptance as the keynote of attitudes about height, I want to point out that sometimes professional medical advice should be sought. Growth is controlled by the pituitary gland which sometimes does not function sufficiently or else overfunctions. We know that the bones of a boy do not set until the sixteenth or seventeenth year and those of a girl do not set until about the twentieth year. Hence indications of too great a deviation in growth—one way or another— should be brought to the attention of a physician. Despite the Biblical dictum, height sometimes *can* be increased by several inches. Likewise disproportionate growth can sometimes be checked. Be quite certain, however, that the deviations warrant such action and are not merely the normal differences shown by all individuals.

What about the too chubby, overweight girls and boys? Here the situation is somewhat different from the situation in regard to height. Obesity in adolescence may have a psychological base. The adolescent may overeat because he—or she—is "hungry" for love and can satisfy that need only at the oral level through eating. In a girl who is obese, there may be an unconscious desire to be like Mother—to have the large belly of pregnancy, the large breasts of the nursing mother. Then, with the realization of how unesthetic it is to be fat, comes a period of dieting, of penance. Obesity is sometimes an indication of hormonal disfunctioning. A physician should be consulted to determine whether the condition is psychological or physical, and his advice should be followed in handling the situation.

In considering the physical difficulties that may create problems in adolescence, we should note lack of motor co-ordination, undue fatigue, and in girls excessive discomfort in menstruation.

Lack of motor co-ordination resulting in awkwardness in gait and in movements of all kinds is a temporary situation that will pass if it is not allowed to loom too large. Simply put, it comes from the lag in retraining muscles that have increased in size as the adolescent grows. If you can keep from scolding Jack when he overturns your favorite table lamp, and are patient with Agnes when she breaks the dishes, this phase of awkwardness will soon be outgrown, as the young people learn to handle themselves. If, however, you make an issue of such things, berate the culprits for clumsiness, it will only increase their awkwardness and may result in withdrawal in order to avoid embarrassing situations.

Fatigue, that feeling of being "tired all the time," is common in adolescence. Some of it, of course, has natural causes— the young persons' excessive activity, the late hours they like to keep in emulating adults, the anxieties inherent in this period of development. Sometimes, however, fatigue is the result of undue anxiety and worry. Emotional upsets drain the adolescent's energy. If you suspect that your young son or daughter is fatigued out of all proportion to the amount of exercise taken and the amount of energy expended, you should seek professional help in getting to the root of the difficulty.

You will recall that I pointed out in discussing menstruation that normally it should not cause discomfort or interfere with a girl's usual pursuits. If your adolescent daughter consistently has headaches, nausea, cramps, and has to go to bed for several days when she menstruates, she should be taken to a gynecologist for examination. The difficulty may be physical. It may be psychological. In either case, find out what is the matter.

Another problem that sometimes arises in adolescent girls is breast development that deviates too greatly from what is considered normal. The flat-chested girl with no bosom to speak of can rectify what she considers her inadequacy with falsies. These stand her in good stead except, of course, when the time comes for petting. The girl with pendulous breasts can also generally help herself to attain a more esthetic appearance by a skillfully fitted bra. Sometimes, the intense feeling of inferiority that comes from having "ugly" pendulous breasts warrants recourse to plastic surgery.

A common physical difficulty in adolescence is skin blemishes. Their cause is well understood, and it is known that they are a passing phase in the normal growth process. Yet they cause anguish and suffering and are responsible for temporary and sometimes permanent personality difficulties.

Simply put, there is in adolescence an increase in the blood supply to the sweat glands on the face, back, shoulder blades, and sometimes other exposed parts of the body. The glands are not yet ready to dispose of the additional amounts of sweat. The secretions clog up the entrance of the glands, bacteria set up infection and inflammation, and the result is blackheads, pimples and acne. You would think that so normal and simple a matter, moreover something that will soon pass away, could be explained to young people.

Perhaps if it were explained, it would not cause so much unhappiness. Boys want to go with girls who will be admired, they don't want to be seen with girls whose skin blemishes make them appear repulsive. And the same is true about girls' estimates of the boys who seem unattractive to them.

Sometimes acne and other skin difficulties are used as a cover-up for some less tangible difficulty. Pat was pretty and she should have been popular, by all external standards. But somehow she didn't click with the boys. She felt herself smarter than most of them, enjoyed taking them down, and flaunting what she thought was her superior learning. Naturally, they left her severely alone.

Came the Junior Prom, which Pat's mother had been dreading, because if past experience counted Pat would get no bids. This wasn't Mother's idea of the kind of girlhood Pat should have. Trying to encourage Pat to put out some strings for a partner, Mother suggested a new dress, phone calls to girl friends with brothers, a small party at home as a come-on. But Pat pushed aside all these ideas. The Prom date came nearer and nearer, until it was one day off. Still no bid. Pat spent the evening alone in her room. She busied herself with taking out blackheads until her face was swollen and angry looking and she was a sight.

"Look at my face," she said, as she appeared at the breakfast table. "It's a lucky thing I'm not going to the dance. I just couldn't have gone, the way I look." She had an alibi to bolster her ego.

Pat was suffering from something more serious than acne. She had purposely made the acne worse, had taken refuge in self-mutilation in order to cover up her lack of popularity and save face. If her mother were wise, she would understand this, and try to get at the cause of the difficulty. If necessary, she would seek professional help before Pat's withdrawals and rationalizations became a fixed pattern.

The adolescent boy or girl who must wear eyeglasses is in a less difficult position today than in former times, thanks to the public relations experts who have given eyeglasses glamour and style and have somehow made it appear desirable to wear them. But there are still many young people who stumble and fumble, unwittingly cut their friends on the street because they cannot see well enough to recognize them, screw up their faces in perpetual squints in a vain attempt to get along without glasses. Sam doesn't want to be called a coward and resents the fact that the boys won't fight with a "four-eyes." Beth doesn't want to be thought a bookworm. Eyeglasses, however, are so common that we really do not consider eye defects a handicap.

Faulty hearing and its rectification with a hearing aid are unfortunately not yet similarly accepted. As hearing aids are made more inconspicuous, smaller and lighter, and more easily worn, a definite trend has set in for accepting them just as eyeglasses are accepted. Mary, who is hard-of-hearing, can take advantage of the clever ways of wearing a hearing aid so that nobody will notice it. If she is more robust, she may prefer to let people see the little "button" (the receiver) and the wire, so that others who are hard-of-hearing will be encouraged to follow suit. In either case, by wearing an aid she will avoid the psychological difficulties that are peculiar to defective hearing.

A person who hears with difficulty often finds it more comfortable to withdraw from social contacts. He is prone to think that people are talking about him when he cannot hear what they say, and becomes suspicious and sensitive. He misses out on plays and lectures, music, church, movies and many other normal pleasures. Parents of children with subnormal hearing should seek competent medical advice. This advice will probably include the use of a hearing aid and lip reading. The latter, though a necessity only for the completely deaf person, is a useful adjunct to hearing. In addition, I am told, it is quite a lot of fun. You can "hear" with your eyes all the best stories told across the aisle in the train or subway, and no one will be any the wiser.

The various physical conditions I have described above are handicaps chiefly if attitudes about them are faulty, or they are situations that will clear themselves up, or defects that can to a large extent be rectified. Many adolescents, however, have serious physical handicaps that must be lived with and adjusted to. Here, even more than in the case of the physically normal adolescent, the parents play a significant role.

One difficulty is that parents have feelings of guilt about their children's illnesses and handicaps, even when they know that they have done everything possible to prevent them. These guilt feelings complicate the situation. They must be acknowledged and handled, if the parents are to do their part.

Jerry, now fifteen, had rheumatic fever during childhood. It left him with a cardiac condition that he must learn to live with. The attitude of his parents is the key to how well he will be able to do so. He has had to lie quiet for long periods; he has had protracted bouts of illness, during which he has been waited on "hand and foot." Because of his illness, he has been treated as an infant, long after he was no longer an infant in years. And so, he may stay in the infant phase, continue in the role of a baby. But it is possible to adjust to the limitations of this physical condition. Jerry has one edge on Johnny, who wears a brace. There is no external sign to his handicap. He— and his parents—must accept the situation. It can be done. There are many sedentary interests and activities for the child and boy who must be physically inactive.

Diabetes is another illness that requires great adjustment in modes of living. In former times, the diabetic was doomed. Today, thanks to the advances in medical knowledge and especially to the discovery of insulin, the diabetic child or adolescent can function normally, with almost as good a life expectancy as anyone else. He must, of course, be under a doctor's care. And he must be taught to exercise self-discipline in carrying out the doctor's orders, adjusting his diet, and taking shots, if these are necessary. Again, the attitude of the parents is all-important. They must somehow impress upon their child the importance of giving himself the care that is necessary for his survival, and at the same time prevent him from being unduly focused on his own health. The literature of diabetes is full of heartening stories of good adjustment to this difficult situation.

Curvature of the spine is less frequent today than formerly, but this condition does occur and must be met, just as other physical handicaps must be met. People tend to avoid those who have physical deformities, through unconscious fear of contagion—illogical as this fear is—or to avoid their own unconscious drive to cripple someone. Thus the boy or girl with curvature of the spine is at a great disadvantage. It must be faced courageously, just as other defects are faced.

Generally the asthmatic adolescent had been an asthmatic child. Asthma results from contraction of the smooth muscles of the bronchi. What makes them contract is more complex. There is general agreement among physicians that many cases of asthma are caused psychologically, and that the attack is used unconsciously (that is, without conscious thought) as a protective device. For some reason the child is filled with hate or fear. He is afraid of being left alone, of being abandoned; he wants to explode, to burst out in angry speech. The asthmatic attack keeps him from doing so. It also keeps him from being left alone, because his mother and others must stay with him and take care of him.

This is a very much simplified statement of a complicated and intricate process. The help of your family doctor, and perhaps at his suggestion, of a psychiatrist, is generally needed. Nevertheless, one piece of advice can be offered here. It is the same, in essence, as that I have given in discussing other physical handicaps. The adolescent boy or girl *and* their parents must squarely face the situation. They must try to understand it and take steps to rectify it.

The problems that must be faced in rearing epileptic and mentally retarded children are perhaps too specialized for discussion in this book. I shall, however, touch upon them briefly.

The epileptic child must be protected in order to prevent bodily injury during seizures. He must be watched because during a seizure he may become a danger to others as well as to himself. Thus the stage is again set for infantile behavior, just as in the faulty handling of the handicaps discussed above. Moreover, other youngsters quite understandably recoil from the sight of an epileptic seizure, with its frightening manifestations. The child becomes resentful and hostile; he takes refuge in being self-centered, rebellious of control, and irritable. Matters are even worse if epilepsy first appears in adolescence. The young boy or girl is frightened—perhaps he will die during seizure. He is withdrawn, ashamed to be seen by his comrades.

Formerly epileptics were generally considered better off in institutions where they could live in a sheltered environment and be trained for occupations within their capacity. Today, medication can cut down and even completely control seizures in about 80 per cent of cases. The epileptic must, however, be under the continuous care of a physician. This modern method of treating epilepsy has been so successful that in some states plans are being made to close the institutions for epileptics.

The mentally retarded adolescent who is struggling to get along in a normal setting will have bouts of explosive irritability. This is his only defense against persons of superior intelligence. Parents of mentally retarded children should seek professional guidance and counsel. Somehow they must face the problem and do whatever is best for themselves and for the other children in the family. Institutional care, where the retarded child can function within the limits of his capacity, is generally, but not always, the best solution. Each situation must be worked out individually.

A helpful booklet issued by the Minnesota Department of Public Welfare, *You Are Not Alone*, says: "Being the mother or the father of a mentally retarded child may be one of the most difficult and challenging experiences that you will ever face. Understanding and acceptance do not come without pain, and even with the advice of specialists, plans take time and are not always easy to work out . . . For your child, the plan that will suit him best. For yourselves, the peace of mind and satisfaction of knowing that you are doing all that you can."

It is the parents' attitude, here as in less tragic handicaps, that is all important. They must be aware of their guilt feelings and come to grips with them; they must try, somehow, not to reject the child.

What general advice can be given to the parents of adolescents (and to the adolescents themselves) in solving the problems arising from physical deviations—imaginary or actual, temporary or permanent? Give your adolescent son and daughter the feeling that however they look, whatever their build, or physical handicap, they have your love and support. Not strangling love that overprotects them and keeps them dependent, but constructive love that helps them live with themselves.

If there is a physical handicap, do your utmost to correct it, and accept what cannot be corrected. Do not cover up your child's defect in your own mind, pretending it does not exist. Face it. Do not let unconscious guilt feelings and hostility toward the child destroy your relationship with him or spill over into hostility toward the outside world. Steer a course between necessary care and the fostering of independence.

If parents act in this way, the adolescent will do his part. He will have the right attitude toward deviations from the normal, and will adjust to and surmount actual physical handicaps.

CHAPTER SEVEN

Adjustment to Parents, Brothers and Sisters

IN THE NORMAL COURSE of development each individual establishes personal relationships in a continuously widening range. His first relationship, as an infant, is with his mother. Then, as infant and child, he reacts to his father, brothers and sisters, other persons in the household and the family, and children at school and at play. By the time adolescence is reached, life has demanded that the young person also establish social relationships of various kinds with other persons young and old— at school, at church, at camp and in all manners of other social settings. Some general idea of what may be called normal relationships has been given in the first part of this book.

The adolescent's capacity to enter into all these relationships, to adjust to the people in his environment, depends chiefly on the relationships established between him and his parents and, to a lesser extent, between him and his brothers and sisters during his formative years.

Sometimes the members of this immediate family circle have personality traits that create problems of adjustment for the adolescent. Sometimes situations beyond anyone's control give rise to difficulties.

I have indicated in previous chapters that children have the best chance for wholesome development when their parents are themselves well-adjusted and mature, and when they have a satisfactory, emotionally sound marriage relationship. If one or both parents have personality difficulties, the child's development is effected adversely, chiefly because such difficulties are likely to manifest themselves in the parents' attitude toward the child. Let us examine the effects of parental domination, submissiveness, rejection and other attitudes on the adolescent boy or girl.

Martin had always felt, even in early childhood, that he was unwanted and unloved. He felt that the whole world was against him and that he could not hold his own with other children. Overwhelmed by anxiety and a sense of his own inferiority, he was suspicious of everyone around him and found it necessary to defend himself against the slightest criticism or insult. By the time Martin reached adolescence, his every act was aggressive. At home he was always fighting with his brothers and sisters, who seemed to him to be favored by his parents. At school he was unruly, in an unconscious effort to gain the teacher's attention. He considered his classmates as rivals and competitors, and so he was constantly battling with them. If his aggressive tendencies are not controlled or turned into more productive channels, the chances are that he will become a delinquent. In Martin's make-up, the elements of hate predominate over the elements of love. His basic drive is to gain whatever end he wants by whatever means he can contrive. It does not matter who gets hurt. Martin does not know that he is the victim of his own aggression, and that it has been created by his parents' openly expressed rejection.

Janie's parents reject her in more subtle ways. They are forever reminding her of how much they love her—witness all that they do for her, and how much they sacrifice themselves for her. "We don't mind the expense of your music lessons, darling," Mother coos. "Daddy and I want to give you everything that will help you." And Father says, with mock gruffness, "If my little daughter has her heart set on camp, then she's going." Janie is supposed to be happy—"That's all we want, darling"—but instead she feels inadequate and guilty. She is confused by the murky emotional atmosphere, the subtle inferences that she should be grateful for all that is done for her. Somehow it's her fault that her mother had to go without a new coat so that she could have a new dress for the school dance. She didn't ask for the dress. She would—almost—have preferred not to have it and be spared this vague feeling that she is ungrateful and must make amends. Janie comes to hate all the things her parents give her—and to hate herself for not accepting them with grateful thanks. Unconsciously she is rejecting these tokens of her parents' love because she is asked to pay too great a price for them.

Some parents put in a bill more openly. Never for a moment is the adolescent allowed to forget all that the parents are doing for him and the return payment that is expected. "After all we have done for you, the least you can do is to work hard at school—the least you can do is to stop wasting your time—the least you can do—" and so on and so on, in a never-ending round. The youngster has no spontaneous, private life. Any infractions of the regulations his parents have meticulously set down for him (or her) call forth reproaches and accusations of ingratitude. He is beset by anxiety, because it seems that he cannot do what is expected of him. And he is also beset by guilt because he feels ungrateful. The parents impress upon him that in gratitude for what they are doing for him he should unquestioningly comply with their wishes. Usually they emphasize the economic sacrifices they are making and explain over and over again that they want to give their child the best possible education. Often the parents exempt their son from all household chores and home responsibilities so that he can devote all his time to study. On the same grounds, they also forbid him to spend any time in social activities. It is

easy to see that in such an environment the adolescent has
little chance for normal development.

In families of some means, where the parents are social
climbers, the externals of the situation are reversed, although
the basic mechanism of "putting in a bill" is the same. Such
parents give their adolescent son or daughter ample spending
money, fine clothes, a car. Unable, fundamentally, to give their
children love, they give them money; they do not realize that
to the adolescent a feeling of being loved is far more essential
than money and what money can buy. These parents, in return
for what they give, demand that the youngster "make the most
of his opportunities," cultivate as friends young people higher
up in the economic and social scale. Here, too, is the devil's
chorus of "the least you can do—" and a constant nagging and
arranging of matters that should be normal outgrowths of the
adolescent's own interest. In this environment, the adolescent
may be overly aggressive. He is likely to have an exaggerated
feeling of his own importance and to ride roughshod over those
who seem to him to be inadequate or subordinate, demanding
that they bow to his wishes. These attitudes also show up in
his relationship with his parents. He feels that if they give him
such an ample allowance and expect him to go with top-drawer
young people they must think he is pretty wonderful. So he
demands that they too look up to him, he treats them with dis-
dain and feels that they are, or should be, subordinate to him.

Parents are sometimes overambitious for their children
and push them beyond their intellectual or physical capacities.
Some adolescents, unable to meet their parents' unrealistic demands and at the same time unable to defend themselves from
the forcefulness of these demands, escape from the dilemma
through a variety of symptoms—severe fatigue, loss of appetite, nausea, insomnia—that have no physical cause. Others are
aggressive toward their parents, and still others, so subdued and

fearful that they cannot protest at home, direct their hostility and anger to their teachers and sabotage their own scholastic progress. All these ways of reacting are responses to a situation that the adolescent cannot meet in any other way.

When Bob came to me for treatment he was getting poor marks at school, he had withdrawn from social activities and complained of severe headaches. His parents, I found out, had set a pace for him that was far beyond his capacity. They wanted him to get all A's at school. They also wanted him to shine in extracurricular activities, to be sought after socially, well-liked by young and old, and always to be a paragon in his conduct. He couldn't live up to their expectations. He became filled with repressed hostility toward his parents and showed it in temper tantrums. His poor marks were a form of unconscious sabotage, a way of taking revenge on them. Bob was escaping from a situation with which he could not cope. He responded to his parents' unrealistic high standards by feeling utterly inadequate, the victim of anxiety and hostility.

All of the types of parents described above actually reject their children. Sometimes they do it quite openly, sometimes they cover up their real attitudes consciously or unconsciously. The causes of parental rejection are complex, and any adequate discussion of them would take us too far afield from our main interest—the adolescent's relations with his parents and the effect of these relations on his development. I want, however, to touch briefly on some of the reasons why mothers reject their children. Sometimes they do so because they love only themselves and have no room in their emotional life, as it were, for their children. Sometimes they have had to give up favored positions in the business or social world to undertake motherhood. They may have had children, not out of love for them, but in an effort to "save" a tottering marriage, or to hold a husband who is insistent in his demands for an heir.

The adolescent boy whose mother has always rejected him has missed a necessary step in his development, and is unable to establish any sort of relationship with a girl, as other boys in his age group are beginning to do. He is full of emotional tension and anxiety, and he is apt to seek emotional satisfaction from men or other boys. The adolescent daughter of a rejecting mother generally has poor relationships with women. Her hostility toward her mother, because she has been deprived of maternal affection, spreads out to include hostility toward all women. Unconsciously, she wants to destroy them and she also fears them for what they may do to her in retaliation. She frequently shows peculiar behavior. For example, she may be afraid to stay at home alone or to travel alone, and thus she forces her mother to stay with her and give her the attention she so sorely needs. Indirectly, she achieves some sort of relationship with her mother and at the same time she punishes her mother for having rejected her.

There is also the mother who has a strong urge to stay forever young. She is really interested only in herself, and her child is just a plaything, an appendage to enhance her own importance. She indulges the youngster and gives him a great deal of attention throughout childhood, not to satisfy his needs but to satisfy her own. Significantly, the child is often called "Baby" well on into adolescence, as if he were not a person in his own right, with a name of his own. By keeping him "a baby," the mother preserves the illusion of her own youth.

The boy who has enjoyed a baby role throughout childhood does not make the usual attempts to be independent and assert himself in adolescence. He actually prefers the dependent role, and even protests when called upon to function on his own. Long after adolescence is past in terms of years, he clings tenaciously to his mother and postpones even thinking about marriage. Many a girl, in a similar baby relationship with her mother, rejects suitor after suitor and refuses to marry because it would mean separation from her mother. The mother who through self-love keeps her child dependent, instead of fostering his (or her) growth and development toward independence, impairs his capacity for a normal healthy love relationship with someone of his own generation. Such children, grown to adulthood in years, remain immature and tend to take refuge in phantasy and daydreaming.

Overdominating parents who supervise their children's every act create problems no less than parents who reject or neglect their children. Bruce had grown up in an atmosphere of discipline and definite commands as to what he was to do at every moment of the day. As a child he responded by being a perfectionist, a fussbudget, and he also responded by having doubts, anxiety and a sense of incompetence, for he was never able to do everything in just the way his parents wanted. As an adolescent, Bruce tried tentatively to reach out for independence, but he was thwarted at every turn and this only increased his sense of inadequacy. His mother opened and read his mail, listened in on his telephone conversations and sat up for him when he went out to parties on Saturday night. No matter how late the hour, she was waiting, first to scold because it was "long after his bedtime" and then to demand a point-by-point account of all that had happened, and to criticize and comment and make suggestions about how he should behave next time. Bruce was torn between his desire for approval and praise from his parents, especially his mother, and his desire to be independent and free of parental authority. So he began to omit from his accounts of his doings anything that would meet with disapproval. He arranged to get his mail at a friend's house, and he practiced other forms of deceit that made life smoother for him. But he paid the price for this conduct by feeling guilty and anxious.

When the time came for Bruce to enter college he man-aged, somehow, to persuade his parents to let him go away from home. Once out of their reach, away from their prying eagle eyes, he reacted to freedom by breaking all rules and regula-tions. Unaccustomed to self-discipline, knowing in his past only discipline imposed on him by his parents, he could not function on his own. He gambled, kept late hours, smoked excessively and slipped from one kind of impulsive and blunder-ing misbehavior to another. Only after Bruce, with psychiatric help, had gained insight into the basis of his conduct was he able to surmount the handicaps of his upbringing.

Not very different from dominating parents are the right-eous ones. Everything is strictly weighed in terms of right and wrong, and somehow whatever the adolescent takes pleasure in—sports, parties, hobbies—is wrong. Rules are laid down by the parents and the adolescent is expected to obey them—and no questions asked. The young boy or girl has no way of doing anything he wants—however innocent—except by subterfuge and secrecy. Before he knows it, he is caught up in a mesh of lies and furtive conduct.

Ann wants to go home with her friend Bess after school and try out a new hairdo, and Sidney wants to watch the chess tournament at the Y and pick up a few points. They know from sad experience that if they ask permission for these normal pastimes it will be denied, and that if they report about them afterwards there will be scoldings and a scene. Much simpler to take refuge in that ever dependable alibi—"I have to go to the library." But lies bring a feeling of guilt, and a need for self-punishment, and these in turn bring on a feeling of hostility toward the parents. Soon Ann and Sidney are in open conflict with their parents, who cannot possibly understand such "ingratitude" since all has been done for "the children's good." In a situation with such cross-purposes, neither side is inclined to be forgiving and a permanent breach in the relationship is apt to result.

Many parents go to the other extreme and are too permissive. Their children have almost unlimited freedom in the home, they do whatever they want regardless of the wishes or comfort of the adults. As adolescents these children are tactless —they have never been trained to consider other people's feelings. They do not learn from their own mistakes—in the past their parents always overlooked mistakes and excused them. Adolescents raised in an environment that is too permissive are so used to getting whatever they want that they cannot understand why any of their demands are opposed. Hence they are ill-prepared for the realities of life. Unaccustomed to authority, they have little respect for their parents and for other adults. They are outwardly assertive and self-reliant. Inwardly they remain dependent upon their parents and other adults because they expect adults to do their bidding, and they are inordinately upset and thrown off balance if this expected pattern is disrupted.

Related to undue permissiveness in rearing children is indulgence and too much solicitousness about them. We know how the mother bird pushes her young out of the protecting nest when they are old enough to fly; how the young ducklings are taught to find food for themselves; and how the bear forces her cubs out of the lair and turns away from them when the time has come for them to be on their own. It is strange that only human beings sometimes do not conform to what seems to be the law of nature for parents. This law is that the young must be protected and nourished while they are helpless, but must be allowed to take care of themselves, indeed must be forced to take care of themselves, when they have outgrown the period of dependency.

Parents are indulgent for various reasons. Some of these

reasons are obvious and command our sympathy and under-standing, if not our approval; others are less obvious. Perhaps the child was born after all hope of parenthood had been abandoned. Perhaps the death of one of their children has focused too much emotion on the surviving child. More diffi-cult to understand is the situation in which the parents seem to be atoning for some vague guilt. Perhaps they did not want the child, or the mother rebelled against pregnancy and at-tempted unsuccessfully to terminate it. When the baby is born, she tries to salve her conscience by overwhelming it with love. Guilt feelings about children, disguised as love and bearing fruit in oversolicitude and indulgence, can arise from many sources.

Peter, the child of indulgent parents, has only a meager chance for normal development. He received little or no train-ing in childhood. Because every whim was satisfied, he as-sumed that he had a right to demand any and everything and that his demands would somehow be satisfied. During adoles-cence Peter is unruly and extremely aggressive, and his aggres-sion does not abate as it does in normal development. He seeks to dominate every situation. Caught at the oral-narcissistic phase of his development, he is incapable of loving another person. He is attracted to girls who, like his mother, spoil and indulge him. Thus his chances of making a happy choice of a wife later on are indeed slim.

Now let us consider some situations that arise more directly from the parents' personality difficulties.

Johnny's father is the boss of the household and proves it by physical force. Even small infractions of the rules he lays down are punished severely. Johnny's mother does noth-ing to defend him or comfort him. She also quails before the tyrant and keeps peace in the family by complete submission to her husband. Johnny fears his father and cannot compete with him—he doesn't even try. To avoid being beaten and to maintain an uneasy truce, he imitates his mother, and is weak, submissive, gentle and feminine in his ways. He is more like a girl than a boy. He understands girls, they like him and treat him like one of themselves. Yet, if Johnny has a special girl, he withdraws if another boy comes along and shows any interest in her, for he cannot stand up to competition.

If the boy is more aggressive than Johnny, he is likely to rebel openly against his father and to defend his mother in the clashes between the parents. He is, however, not kind and loving toward his mother. He berates her for allowing his father to be "bossy" and at the same time he is equally bossy. He is assertive at home, not because it gets him anywhere—indeed it usually results in his being mauled by his father—but because he enjoys asserting himself. His antagonism to his father is extended into antagonism against all men and into rebellion against all authority. He is an isolated, bitter, anti-social boy—hostile to men and other boys, despising pleasant submissive girls who are too much like his mother and hating aggressive girls who won't "stand for his gaff."

What happens to a girl in a similar set up? Doris, who lives in this kind of home, rather looks down on her mother. Since her infancy her father has been strongly attached to her, and in early adolescence he devoted all his leisure to her. Doris has never felt that her mother threatened her relationship with her father. She has shoved Mother aside and taken first place with Father. It is father and daughter, not husband and wife, who discuss business affairs and make decisions. The daughter is the head of the household when her father is away, and the mother submissively takes the subordinate position. Doris, identifying with her father, develops into a strong masculine type of girl. She can brook no competition and must always be the leader. The idea of working *with* others, or *under* others, is totally incomprehensible to her. She must always be on top, dominating all people with whom she comes in contact. If Doris finally marries, the chances are she will select a man who is weak, like her mother, for her drive to dominate is carried over into adult life.

It goes without saying that not every girl who has a bossy father and a sweet, quiet, submissive mother reacts in this way. The daughter in such a home may be strong and masculine, like Doris, but her unconscious guilt feelings for having pushed her mother into the background result in a deep sympathy for her mother and anger at her father. To make amends and overcome her guilt, she attempts to make Mother happy and is likely to stay strongly attached to her for most of her life. If she marries she will probably select a weak man, just as Doris does, but in all likelihood she will want to live with her mother, or at least near her, so that she can continue to look after her. Still another reaction is for the daughter to identify with her submissive mother to such an extent that she is herself submissive, anxious and emotionally tense. Because the father is bossy, she is afraid of him and unable to make a close and affectionate contact with him in middle adolescence. Since she has missed the necessary experience of a father-daughter relationship, she will probably be unable to develop any kind of relationship with boys and will stay fixed at the homosexual level of development. Sometimes she escapes from reality into mental illness.

What of the opposite situation, the home in which the mother is overly aggressive and the father too submissive? The mother plays the male role—wears the pants, as the inelegant but expressive saying goes. If there are two sons in such a home, the elder is likely to be a weakling, dancing attendance on his mother, trying to please her by being subservient. He seeks her attention and love by playing the woman to her "maleness." Yet he is confused by his two roles as a male and a "female," and may escape from this conflict through phantasy. If he cannot do this successfully, he may escape into mental illness. The younger son does not, in general, follow the same pattern. He is self-sufficient and not the victim of the mother's drive for power and maleness. This drive, it seems, is satisfied by having her first-born at her beck and call. Thus the second son escapes the hazards that overwhelm his elder brother.

Betty, the daughter of an overly aggressive woman, has little or no opportunity to attach herself to her father, because he is an ineffectual nobody in the family setup, not someone she can look up to. She may try to emulate her mother, and even go her one better in being bossy and masculine. She will not be interested in boys. She will scorn dances and parties and pretty clothes. Sometimes the situation is distorted in a sad and disturbing way. The girl may scorn her femininity as something worthless, and since it is worthless she may see no reason to safeguard it. So she readily drifts into promiscuity. She may become promiscuous in vague defiance at her lot. In effect, her unconscious thoughts run like this: "I don't really want to be a woman; look at Mother—she's just like a man. I can't do anything about it, so I'll just show them that the woman part of me is of no consequence. It means nothing to me. . . ."

If both parents are bossy and aggressive, the adolescent boy and girl may vacillate between aggressiveness and weakness. They are seeking affection and love from the parent of the opposite sex—the boy from his mother, the girl from her father—and they are foredoomed to failure. So they dart hither and thither, trying to gain their objective, first by one approach, then by another. At one moment they stand up for their rights —copying the behavior of the parents. At another, they are weak and humble, fearful of making mistakes, almost apologizing for being alive. The parents, driven by their desire for power and by their own stubborn need to manage everything and everybody, are probably unaware of what is going on, completely without understanding of the inconsistent behavior of their harassed youngsters. They brush off all the pathetic—and futile—attempts at establishing satisfying emotional relationships.

The situations I have sketched are, of course, oversimplified. Human beings have intricate and sometimes contradictory traits, and life is not so neatly put into categories. Furthermore, these situations by no means cover all personality difficulties and their combinations. The general patterns, however, are clear. The parents' personality traits and their attitudes toward their children may give rise to problems of adjustment in the relationship between the adolescent and his parents, and may impede the adolescent's normal development.

Does one of the situations I have described resemble your own in some respects? Do you see yourself in one of these parents? If you ponder these questions, you may get a clue to where you are going astray and to why you are not as good a parent as you want to be—and can be. I believe that if you understand how your attitude as a parent and your own personality difficulties affect your son or daughter, you will try to change yourself. If you cannot handle your difficulties unaided, do not hesitate about getting help from a psychiatrist.

We must now consider how the death of the father or mother affects the adolescent boy and girl. If you as a reader have suffered the loss of your spouse, you are carrying a heavy burden and I have no wish to make it heavier by adding anxiety to your sorrow. But in this situation, as in so many others, difficulties are lessened by knowledge and understanding. I purposely do not focus on the immediate emotional impact of the parent's death on the adolescent, but rather on the psychological difficulties that arise when the initial mourning period has passed. I hope that an awareness of these matters will help you and your adolescent son or daughter.

The father's death affects the adolescent boy and the adolescent girl in different ways, and for each of them the effects are different according to whether the adolescent is in the early, middle or late phase of adolescence when the loss occurs. The mother's death has quite different impacts on the adolescent. Here, too, the effects are dissimilar for a boy and for a girl, and further dissimilar according to the phase of his or her development.

You will gain some understanding of these effects and why they differ in all these ways if you think about the psychological development of adolescent boys and girls in the normal home setup of father-mother-son and father-mother-daughter, as I described it in the first part of this book.

In early adolescence, you will recall, the father is an important figure in the boy's life. The boy looks up to his father, admires him and feels protected and secure. He identifies himself with his father and tries to copy his manly traits. The boy whose father dies during or shortly before this phase feels left out in the cold when his comrades speak boastingly of what their fathers do, and of how clever, strong and capable they are. More important, the father's death deprives the boy of an essential companionship, a step in his journey toward adulthood. As a result, he may remain a preadolescent child, psychologically speaking. Fortunately, however, it is possible for him to establish this essential relationship with some other man. This often happens, you will recall, even when the father is living but for some reason cannot fill this role in his son's life. When a boy's father has died, there are many people who can take his place—an older brother, an understanding uncle or grandfather

—it does not matter whether they come from the mother's or
the father's side of the family—a male teacher, scoutmaster,
club director. If the mother remarries at this time, the stepfather can readily be accepted as a substitute father and a satisfactory relationship can be established between man and boy.
The mother, in any case, can mitigate the effects of the father's
death by understanding her son's special need at this time and
by fostering his attachment to a father substitute.

Adjustment is not so readily made to the loss of the father
in the boy's middle adolescent period. In this period, you will
recall, the boy's attention is focused on his mother and he feels
that the father is a rival for the mother's attention and love.
If the father dies at this time or shortly before, the boy has in
effect disposed of his rival and triumphed over him. Yet he
cannot enjoy this easy victory. There is inner conflict and guilt
because his unconscious wish to eliminate the father has been
granted. The boy is likely to quickly abandon the activities
that are normal for his age and try to be an adult before his
time. Attempting to stand in his father's place, he may insist on
leaving school and going to work to support his mother. He is
likely to be possessive about her and to resent any attention she
gets from other men. If she remarries he will feel that the stepfather is a rival and will probably be openly hostile toward
him. This hostility and resentment of the man who has come
between him and his mother is likely to persist. You will recall
that normally the boy's attachment for the mother gives way
to interest in girls. When the father has died, this attachment—
too easily established and maintained as the only male in the
picture—may be so strong that the normal shift to interest in
contemporaries does not take place. The son may remain a
bachelor, "devoted to his mother," or he may later on marry an
older woman who in effect substitutes for the mother. Sometimes his normal development is merely slowed up, and in his

early twenties he passes through the experiences that under ordinary circumstances he would pass through in middle adolescence.

By late adolescence the boy is interested in girls and his attraction to his mother and need for love from her is waning, if he has progressed in a normal manner. Thus the father's death at this time, although depressing for him, does not interfere with his basic psychological development. Unfortunately, the late adolescent frequently retains some of the emotional characteristics of middle adolescence. In this case, the father's death may affect him in much the same way as it affects a boy in middle adolescence.

How does the mother's death affect the adolescent boy? Here, as in the case of the father's death, he reacts differently in early, middle and late adolescence.

In early adolescence the boy is primarily interested in his father, and almost any woman who has a motherly attitude and looks after the youngster's physical needs can act as a mother substitute. An older sister, an aunt, a warmhearted housekeeper or maid can fill the role. Sometimes, however, the boy has been too closely identified with his mother. He may then take on passive feminine traits instead of developing in a normal way. If the father remarries at this time, the boy will accept the new wife as a mother substitute.

Matters are not so simple if the mother dies during the boy's middle adolescence. Because he is deprived of the experience of being in love with Mother as an essential steppingstone to interest in girls, he is likely to have difficulty in establishing any kind of relationships with girls or in adjusting to women later in life. Sometimes an older woman can to some extent be the mother substitute and fill this gap but the relationship that is established is, of course, not identical and is not entirely adequate. The mother's death may make the boy try to fill her role in making the father happy and he may then take on many feminine traits. This situation may result in latent or overt homosexuality. If the father remarries at this time, the boy who has formed too close a relationship with the father will resent the stepmother. But if an overly emotional relationship between father and son has not been established, the stepmother is often able to serve as a mother substitute. There is, however, one essential difference between this relationship and the one he would have had with his own mother—the boy does not have an incest taboo in his "wooing" of this "mother."

The mother's death during a boy's late adolescence may speed up his interest in girls and his attachment to a particular girl, but it does not fundamentally affect his psychological development. If the father remarries, the boy makes a satisfactory adjustment to the stepmother, and can develop a close and loving feeling for her. The situation, however, may get out of hand because there is no incest taboo as in the case of the natural mother. Hence the boy may see his father as his successful rival for possession of the stepmother and may show open hostility toward him. As I noted above, some of the emotional characteristics of middle adolescence are frequently retained in the succeeding period. When this happens, the late adolescent boy reacts to his mother's death as if he were in the middle adolescent phase.

Let us now consider how the father's or mother's death affects the adolescent girl. In early adolescence the girl is primarily interested in her mother. She has affectionate feelings for her father; his presence gives her a comfortable sense of belonging to a close-knit family group and it also gives her equal status among her peers. In a deep psychological sense, however, the father is not essential at this time. Hence, baldly put, his death does not have much effect on the girl's psychological development. Should the mother remarry, the new father is accepted with ease.

In middle adolescence, however, the loss of the father has far-reaching effects on a girl. She may have difficulty in establishing satisfactory relationships with boys and later with men, since she has missed the essential step of love and attachment to her father. These difficulties, however, are not as great as those faced in the comparable situation by the middle adolescent boy when his mother dies, chiefly because it is easier for a girl to find father substitutes. Thus she may feel attracted to much older men instead of being interested in boys, and only gradually retrace her steps, as it were, and make contact with her peers. She may try to take her father's place and become too concerned about her mother and too attached to her, to the detriment of her own development. Should the mother remarry at this time, the girl establishes a relationship with her stepfather that is much the same as she would have made with her own father. It differs however, in one respect. Since she is not held back by the incest taboo, she may become too emotionally involved, and this may result in hostility between mother and daughter, and also in conflicts and embarrassing situations with the stepfather.

The girl in late adolescence is not greatly affected by the loss of her father since by this time her interest is normally focused on boys. Her concern for her mother, however, and her feeling that she must take care of her may retard her in establishing relationships with men. Her attachment to the mother may be so strong that it leads her to the postponement of marriage. If the mother remarries, the girl does not generally enter into any fundamental relationship with her stepfather, since she is normally beyond the period of needing it.

She feels chiefly relief at no longer carrying the sole responsibility for her mother's happiness.

Loss of the mother during a girl's early adolescence has much the same affect on her as the mother's loss has on a boy in the same period. Whatever warmhearted woman is at hand to manage the household can be a mother substitute, and the father can also fill this role as well as his own. If the father remarries, the stepmother is acceptable as a mother substitute. In middle adolescence the mother's death accentuates the girl's natural attachment for her father. She has some guilt feelings but they are not as intense as those that disturb a boy in the comparable situation of his father's death. The reason for the difference is perhaps that the girl can take the mother's place in a practical and realistic way in running the household, and that the boy's sense of taking his father's place is more nebulous. The girl in middle adolescence bitterly resents her father's remarriage since it means to her that another woman has usurped her place in his affections. She may repudiate the father by going to live with a neighbor, aunt or grandmother, or by running away and breaking all connection with her family. She may even take revenge on him by becoming promiscuous. If the girl's identification with the mother has been too intense and she feels repudiated and dethroned by the stepmother, she may become mentally ill.

The girl in late adolescence reacts to her mother's death largely in terms of how far along she is in her own development. If she has by this time become detached emotionally from her father and is interested in boys and her own affairs, the mother's death has little basic impact. In this case, if her father remarries, she accepts the new wife in a friendly way without making an emotional contact. But matters work out differently if the girl is still attached to her father and has taken over her mother's role. Then she may devote herself to him and have no interest in boys. If he remarries she will resent the woman who, she feels, is an interloper.

We must consider briefly the situation of orphans. If the child is orphaned while very young and is adopted, then to all intents and purposes he has the same chance for normal development that he would have with natural parents. It is essential, however, that he be told at an early age that he is adopted. If this fact is kept from him, he will surely hear it inadvertently from outsiders and suffer from shock and loss of confidence in the foster parents. The loss of both parents in adolescence is such a terrible tragedy that there generally are relatives, friends, godparents or neighbors willing to take over and do what they can to help the young boy or girl. The adolescent still needs and still wants the guiding hand, the love and protection of parents, and he gratefully accepts whatever provision is made for his welfare. He is thus able to love those who have come to his rescue with a minimum of hostility, and to redirect his love from the parents who are gone to the loving substitutes.

The breakup of a family through divorce or separation also deprives the child of one parent. The absence of one parent affects the adolescent's psychological development in somewhat the same way as the loss of the father or mother through death. There are, however, added complications. In a broken marriage there is usually resentment and bitterness, and a tendency for each of the two people involved to blame the other one for what has happened. In the conflict between the two parents the child is often enlisted as an ally by the parent with whom he lives. His mother may give him a distorted picture of his father as the "guilty party," or his father in similar fashion may try to destroy his confidence in his mother. Loving both parents, the child is torn by conflicting loyalties. Needing for his own development to admire both parents, he is confused and disturbed.

These are only some of the difficulties into which divorce thrusts the children. Even under the best conditions, when the divorced parents are fair-minded and mature, a broken home is tragic and disruptive for the children. Its ill effects, however, can be minimized if the parents are aware of the forces that may mar and scar their children. As in the absence of one parent by death, an effort must be made to provide a substitute parent for the one who is no longer at hand; better still, contact between the child and this absent parent should be fostered and maintained. Each parent should meticulously avoid derogatory attitudes, expressed or unexpressed, about the other one. All these matters can be worked out if the divorced parents can separate their feelings as adults whose marriage has gone on the rocks—whatever the reason—from their feelings as parents and their acceptance of joint responsibility for their children's welfare.

Up to this point I have discussed the adolescent's adjustment to his parents. He has also, throughout childhood, been establishing various kinds of relationships with his brothers and sisters. It is important to consider these brother-sister relationships in detail and to discuss the elements in the family setup that affect them and also affect the child's own personality.

The position of a child in the family—whether first-born, second, youngest, and so on—is a strong factor in his personality make-up. Also important are the attitudes of the parents, their pleasure or disappointment, as the case may be, in the child's being a boy or a girl, their satisfaction or disappointment in the child's looks, intelligence and capacities.

The first-born is faced with situations that may produce

personality difficulties. Whether the child's coming was planned or not planned, the mother is likely to be tense and overanxious during his infancy because of inexperience and doubt as to her capabilities. This situation can often be alleviated by a tactful grandmother, a pediatrician, helpful neighbors and one or two good popular books on infant care. When the first-born turns out to be an only child, both parents tend to overindulge him and to respond with undue concern to every minor ailment. Their anxiety becomes his anxiety. Thrown into more direct and continuous contact with the mother than a child who must share her attention with other children in the family, the only child tends to take on the mother's attitudes and ways of thinking. He does not have the normal and healthy give-and-take that is found in families with brothers and sisters, and as a result he tends to be grown up before his time. Being an only child, however, is not in itself an insolvable problem. It becomes one only through the attitude of the parents.

When other children are born into the family, the first-born also must make adjustments. It is easy to understand his resentment toward the second child who, it seems to him, has displaced him as the center of his parents' interest and affection. I have described earlier in this book the first child's reversion to baby behavior when the new baby arrives, and how his wetting, insistence on again drinking from a bottle, and other behavior difficulties are all efforts to regain the mother's attention. Here we need only note that he has a sense of rivalry with the second-born and that he may take on an attitude of superiority in an effort to compensate for his displacement.

And what of the second child? He often has a secret ambition to equal and outstrip the older child. Indeed, it is natural for the two children to have strong feelings of hostility toward each other. The story of Cain and Abel is the classic example of this sibling rivalry. The third child, if of the same sex as the two older children, may seem to the parents to be a superfluous addition to the family. Even if the parents do not have this attitude, the child may feel that he is superfluous and rejected by the parents. On the other hand, he has an advantage over the second and middle child, for in a family of three boys or three girls the first and third usually band together "against" the middle child. If, however, the third child is a girl with two older brothers or a boy with two older sisters, then the two children of the same sex form an alliance and the third child is in the difficult position of being left out in the cold.

It would be impracticable—and a bit boring, I fear—to go into the many combinations of the number of children in a family and the sex of each child in relation to the sex of the other children. Suffice to say that these combinations are factors in the relationships established between brothers and sisters.

I have tried to make clear in the foregoing discussion that it is normal for brothers and sisters to be jealous and hostile toward one another during childhood. By the time adolescence is reached, however, these feelings have generally been mastered and repressed. They have not, it should be remembered, been eliminated. It is therefore not surprising that in later life, despite sincere affection between siblings, disagreements tend to manifest themselves from time to time.

The rivalries of early childhood are not to be deplored. The adjustments that they demand serve a useful purpose, for the patterns laid down in the relations between brothers and sisters affect the adolescent's social attitudes and the way in which he adjusts to other people. Moreover, these childhood patterns determine the relationships that he will establish in the adult world.

CHAPTER EIGHT

Adjustment to the Outer World

As we have seen in the foregoing chapter, relationships with parents, brothers and sisters are established in childhood and are determining factors in a child's emotional development. The family is at hand to advise and support the child, and by the very nature of his dependence he accepts guidance and protection. The situation changes in adolescence. The young person is caught between two forces—the attitudes of the family and the attitudes of his contemporaries. One of his chief problems is how to adjust to the outside world and particularly to boys and girls of his own age.

To be socially acceptable and on a par with his peers he feels that he must conform to their customs and attitudes, even when this line of conduct leads him into ways that are not acceptable to his parents. The teen-age boy wears dungarees if the other fellows wear them, and the teen-age girl wears blue jeans if the other girls wear them; these are "musts," no matter what the folks at home and the teachers at school think about this way of dressing. Similarly, if everyone in the crowd talks jive and prefers slang to a more conventional way of speaking, then the adolescent boy and girl will also talk this way despite vehement parental protests. Nothing much is at stake and if the parents are wise they will not make an issue of such harmless manifestations of the desire to conform.

Other and more complex problems, however, arise from this desire or, more accurately, this need to conform. It is not always possible for the adolescent to keep in step with his contemporaries. An adjustment of some kind must then be made if the individual—as an adolescent and later as an adult—is to function in society.

Differences in economic status create one of the chief difficulties in the adolescent's adjustment to his peers. The majority of children and young people in America go to publicly supported grammar and high schools, and there is no artificial separation into different schools according to the family income, as in some countries. As a result, boys and girls from wealthy homes, middle income homes and low income homes all go to school together. This situation has many advantages and is perhaps one of the most important factors in developing the unique American attitude that every man is as good as his neighbor, and in building a democratic society. It also gives rise to problems of adjustment in adolescence that should be faced and clearly understood.

The wealthier boys and girls have better clothes, of course, and more spending money than their poorer companions. They tend to band together and look down on the less well-dressed youngsters who have to count every penny to make their weekly allowances last. The more fortunate youngsters may act smug and feel superior, they may brag about what they have and the others do not have. Such attitudes often persist and carry over into adult relationships.

The less well-off young folks, particularly the girls, may develop equally disastrous attitudes. The girl who is noticeably less well-dressed than her comrades often feels inferior and her sense of inadequacy shows up not only in her relations with her schoolmates but also in poor classroom work. She is likely to envy the more fortunately situated girls. In school she suppresses her feelings and may even take on a submissive role in the hope of being accepted by "the crowd," but at home she probably releases her anger. She is unruly and antagonistic and upbraids her parents because their lack of ample means deprives her of things she feels she must have in order to be on an equal footing with the other girls.

Bernice stormed and wept at home and acted as if she were the victim of a major tragedy because her clothes were less pretty than those of her classmates and her allowance was skimpy. Her parents, wanting her to be happy, sacrificed more important things and used their money to buy her stylish clothes and to give her an ample allowance. Although Bernice was now well-dressed and had enough pocket money, she still did not feel on an equal footing with her wealthier classmates. She refused invitations to their homes, lest she be expected to return their hospitality. If she asked these girls to her home, they would see how shabby it was. She was sailing under false colors to no avail. Moreover, her attempts to run with the favored group cut her off from close contacts with girls of her own economic level. And she also felt guilty because she knew that her parents, under pressure, had spent money on her that should have been used for more necessary things. So Bernice belonged nowhere; she was a self-made outcast because she could not face reality. Her difficulties in adjustment were rooted in her lack of a true sense of values, and in her failure to come to grips with the inescapable fact that some people have more money than others. At bottom, her false values were the product of her parents' false values, their failure to have— and to give their daughter—a feeling of true worth that is not dependent on money.

The importance of such feelings is illustrated by what happened to David and Frank, "poor" boys from the Midwest who came to Harvard on scholarships. Their families had nothing to spare for allowances, and both boys had a thin time. They had to scrimp, do their own laundry, watch their pennies, and forego dances, football games and other social activities that called for an outlay of cash. David thrived on the regime. He gleefully learned to iron his shirts and press and mend his well-worn suits. He ferreted out all the enticing things that could be done for free, he did good work and soon had a circle of friends. Frank, on the other hand, was ashamed of his poverty, he was envious of his more prosperous classmates, lonesome and morose. And these attitudes so pervaded his mind that he did poor work and finally lost his scholarship.

Why did these two young men react so differently to the same circumstances? The answer is simple. David's father was a Baptist minister; he was poor, as Baptist ministers are in small towns, but he was honored and respected and the family was looked up to by the entire community. David's parents had given him a true sense of values that did not equate worth with money. Frank, however, came from a family of strivers. The father, urged on by his wife's social ambitions, had flitted from one get-rich-quick job to another, and each one was a bit shady. Frank had grown up in a family that spent all its energies regretting that it was poor and envying those who were better off. No wonder that he thought money not only desirable but essential to happiness.

What of the other side of the picture? Sometimes girls or boys from wealthy homes commendably choose their friends without regard for their economic status. They seek out classmates with whom they have common interests and make close attachments to boys and girls "from the other side of the tracks." If the parents are social climbers, they are likely to object to such democratic attitudes and put pressure on their children not to "waste their time" with people who will be of "no help" in their climb up the social ladder. Here, as in my stories of Frank and Bernice, it is the parents' attitudes that create the difficulties in adjustment.

A boy from a wealthy family often uses his ample allowance to treat the crowd—to buy the sodas and the movie tickets, the admission to the skating rinks, and the like. He is generally not motivated by generosity but by uncertainty about his own worth. He is trying to buy friendship and to win the role of leader with money. If for some reason he no longer has the funds to play this game, his so-called friends probably abandon him, and he learns that friends cannot be bought but must be won through the giving of self.

Many adolescents who could afford to dress well do not do so because they want to avoid being conspicuous among their comrades. Their reasons may be less forthright. They may be unconsciously motivated by a wish to pull down and belittle their parents, and they try to do this by not enjoying what the parents can provide.

In considering the problems that arise from differences in clothes among adolescent girls, it should be remembered that money is not necessarily needed in rectifying the situation. Any woman knows that, in this day of inexpensive copies of high-priced dresses, the ingenious girl with a sense of style can be pretty well turned out on a small dress allowance. Then, too, home economics courses have stimulated girls to make their own clothes, and they can be quite lovely.

Although the situations I have sketched give rise to problems that are serious for the adolescent, it is well to remember—and to remind your adolescent son and daughter—that the economic status of both individuals and families changes rapidly in America. Popular sayings, such as "three generations from shirt sleeves to shirt sleeves" and "yesterday's day laborer is tomorrow's millionaire," as well as popular books of the *Father Struck It Rich* type indicate our belief that financial position is not static and that the lines that divide people into economic groups are not fixed.

Religious and racial groups, however, are another matter. Here prejudices enter the picture and the adolescent's problems of adjustment to contemporaries of other religious faiths, other races or other national backgrounds are not readily solved. Prejudice is a deep-rooted feeling arising from complex causes. Fundamentally these causes are psychological, although they are rationalized in many ways.

Briefly and simply put, the psychological basis of prejudice is lack of understanding of the person against whom the prejudice is directed and, by extension, lack of understanding of the group to which he belongs. This is the way matters work out. We are thrown in contact with a person who seems quite alien to us—in looks or language or social customs or religious beliefs. We cannot understand his way of doing things and so we think of him as mysterious. It is a short and easy step, and a comfortable one, too, from thinking of this person as having mysterious qualities to thinking of him as having detrimental and dangerous qualities and as someone to be avoided. Awe and suspicion are difficult to handle, for they make us feel inadequate and inferior. It is natural to want to overcome such feelings. In doing so, we unconsciously distort facts and add impressions of our own that are rationalizations of why this alien person should be ostracized. As a defense against our own discomfort and insecurity, we feel hostile toward him, we condemn and debase him.

Expand this process of how we think and feel about a person who is "different" to how we think and feel about his group, and you have in very oversimplified terms an explanation of the psychological mechanisms of prejudice. Consider the many ways in which other groups are unlike your own and how facts and impressions can be entangled, and you have some inkling of the devious rationalizations that give a semblance of logic to prejudice. The more insecure a person is, and the more he is frustrated in expressing his inner aggression, the greater will be his prejudice against people who are different.

In the areas where prejudice complicates adolescents' problems of adjustment, their own attitudes are reinforced by the prejudices of their parents and their social group. Young children are not aware of differences in religious beliefs. They play together quite oblivious to the fact that their parents worship in different ways. But as they grow older, discussions at home give them the notion that perhaps people of a different faith are suspect. Mother may remark, quite casually, "Of course I could never be friends with Mrs. B., she's a Catholic," or Father, telling some long story of a business deal, says, "The Jews certainly know how to drive a hard bargain." The idea that people are divided according to religious belief has taken hold, the seeds of prejudice have been sown. Sunday school and attendance at church or temple or synagogue draw children away from their early association with one another. Barriers are set up between them. It is more comfortable to stay with one's own kind within these barriers. Especially in small communities, where the young people's social life generally centers in the church and where each person's religious affiliation is known, the line of least resistance is for adolescent boys and girls to associate with contemporaries of their own faith. Usually anyone who attempts to break through the barrier and become intimate with someone of a different faith runs the risk of being isolated by his own co-religionists.

In summarizing the psychological basis of prejudice above, I said that it begins with a feeling of awe and suspicion about people who do alien things that we cannot understand. It is easy to see how such feelings arise among adolescents of different faiths, and how they strengthen the barriers that divide young people. The Catholic boy follows customs and rituals that are strange to outsiders. He eats fish on Friday, he goes to Mass on Sunday and is familiar with a ritual that is meaningless to the uninitiated. Meeting the parish priest on the street he addresses him as "Father," and does not seem intimidated by his strange robes. To him the priest is a respected and trustworthy friend, the kindly, all-wise father substitute. To the other boys, especially to the Jewish boy if he comes from a family in which the grandparents, perhaps, still tell tales of pogroms, the priest is a mysterious figure, strange and awesome. Following the pattern I have indicated, the non-Catholic boys are very likely to carry over this sense of something strange and somewhat inimical into their attitudes toward all Catholic boys and Catholics in general. Similarly, Jewish boys seem mysterious and strange to their contemporaries of other faiths. Jewish boys, it is whispered, "don't eat ham or oysters, they don't kneel when they pray, they put on shawls and little caps at church." Soon the easy step is taken from feelings of strangeness and mystery to feelings of hostility and suspicion, and from having such feelings about particular boys to having them about the group to which they belong.

Generally hostility is openly expressed when an adolescent of one faith wins something that was desired by an adolescent of a different faith. The two boys have been competing for a job, a prize, victory in the hundred-yard dash, any competition, it matters not what. The loser cannot accept the outcome as "a fair fight and the best man won." It is easier to salve his hurt feelings and protect his self-esteem by blaming his failure on some trick of the victor. He makes some derogatory remark about this and about the victor's religious group. The noxious weed of prejudice has begun to grow. And it continues to grow because each group is trying to cover up its own feelings of inferiority by belittling individuals of another group. In each group, there is a feeling of being threatened by the outsiders—the inferior groups—and of having to put up a defense. Distortions, half-truths and falsehoods are all mingled in the ammunition that is used.

The tragedy is that there is no need for fighting. But the false ideas that adolescents of one faith harbor about contemporaries of another are difficult to eradicate. One step in this direction is for adolescents and their parents to try to understand the forces that create prejudice. Another is to inculcate the idea that all religions have in common the ideals of love and virtue, of living according to the Golden Rule and the Ten Commandments. Interfaith movements which foster mutual understanding of the various faiths and emphasize mutual interests are doing good service in counteracting religious prejudice. The task, however, is enormous, for prejudice in adolescence is fortified by prejudice in the adults with whom the young person is in close contact. Thus it persists into adulthood, where it fortifies the prejudices of the next generation.

The adolescent must also make adjustments to contemporaries of other races and other national backgrounds. Here, too, prejudice distorts his relationships and raises barriers between groups. Prejudice because of race or national origin has the same basic psychological causes as religious prejudice. If you understand the forces that are at work in one kind of prejudice you will be able to understand them in another area.

Before immigration was restricted in the 1920s, large numbers of immigrants came to the United States from the various nations of Europe and to a lesser extent from other parts of the world. Their customs and behavior, their language and looks at first set each national group apart from the earlier arrivals who had already been assimilated and become "Americans." The isolation of each group, generally accentuated by a language barrier and by poverty, tended to make its members cling together, thus reinforcing their strangeness and differences. We tend to forget that each "most recent" immigrant group was a special target for prejudice. The Germans and the Irish were once looked down on, ridiculed as the Dutch and the Micks; prejudice then focused on the Slavs (Hunkies), the Swedes (Squareheads), and the Italians (Wops), and so on. Today the Puerto Ricans who huddle together in our large cities are the victims of prejudice since they are the newest immigrants.

The prejudice that has set up barriers against all these national groups one after the other, and has waned as each group became assimilated, follows the pattern I have described above in discussing religious prejudice. The rationalizations are, of course, different. We should keep in mind that all of us in America with the exception of the Indians are immigrants. Will Rogers, proud of his Indian blood and annoyed at the airs of the Colonial Dames and the D.A.R., put the matter in a nutshell when he said, "Their ancestors may have come over on the *Mayflower*, but mine were already here waiting to meet the boat." Rogers, of course, was revealing his own prejudices in these words. Each incoming group has something to contribute to our national life. Their customs and traditions should not be crushed out; they should be used—indeed they have been used —to enrich our national culture.

One more area of prejudice remains to be discussed, race prejudice against fellow Americans who are Negroes. This subject is so much in the public mind at the present time that little needs to be added here except to emphasize that the psychological basis of prejudice is the same in this field as in others. Let us remember and teach our children that all human beings are "the sons of Adam" and brothers, whatever the color of their skin. The sun shines on all of us, and we are all the children of God. If we can hold fast to this idea, racial prejudice will some day be rooted out. Somehow an adjustment will be made and the race problem—one of the most serious problems faced by Americans—will somehow be solved.

The adolescent's adjustment in the vast and complex areas of prejudice is difficult and cannot—I am forced to admit—be made by the individual alone. It may have to wait for a general improvement in our social attitudes.

A far simpler kind of adjustment is that which must be made between adolescents and the adults around them—the neighbors next door and down the street, the community as a whole. In this instance it is the adults who should do most of the adjusting. Because some young boys ride around in hot rods, people jump to the conclusion that every young person riding at a good speed is a demon and peril on the road. Actually, young people who have been around cars all their lives are generally good drivers and handle a car far better than their elders who probably learned to drive after they were grown up. Because some young people whoop it up with singing and shouting when coming home from a party, people think that every young girl and boy on the streets after midnight is a rowdy headed straight for a life of crime. Often in a discussion between an adolescent and an adult, the latter suddenly pulls his rank and expects the youngster to be submissive and defer to him. If the young man asserts himself, he is accused of being impudent.

The adolescent is often unable to cope with these adult attitudes. In an atmosphere of constant criticism, he may develop anxiety and withdraw from normal activities; he may pretend to be stupid just to keep out of trouble, or he may raise hell just because this is what is expected of him. Girls more often than boys sometimes try to maintain their status and reassure themselves by being verbose, and they use continuous talking about nothing at all as a defense against critical adults. Boys, it seems, have more active ways of gaining attention and combating criticism. If the device of verbosity, of "yakety yak," is successful, it may become an established pattern; and it is then apt to persist into adulthood.

My advice to uncles and aunts, parents' friends, neighbors, storekeepers and all grownups who have any kind of contact with adolescents is simple. Believe and expect the best, not the worst, from the adolescent. In situations that start on an equal footing, maintain that footing; do not shift, when it is to your advantage, to the role of the older person who demands obedience and respect. Do not expect adolescents to do all the adjusting. Some of it is up to you. Let them alone and—with time—they will come out all right.

The adolescents of today are faced with one group of adjustment difficulties that is directly related to the time in which we live. They know little or nothing about a world at peace. From earliest childhood they have heard of war and preparation for war, of fighting and the threat of fighting, of military aggression, defensive alliances among nations. They cannot even imagine a world in which people do not talk about air raids and bombers, beachheads, LSTs, attack and counterattack, casualties, POWs, brainwashing, and so on. Over the entire world hangs the threat of atomic war and of mass annihilation.

Reared in this atmosphere of foreboding and uncertainty, the adolescent boy must adjust to his years of military service. In former times, the boy about to graduate from high school made definite plans for a job or further education. Today, because he knows that he must do his stint in the Army or other branch of the Services, he is likely to drift. There seems to be little use in making plans for the future when he is soon to be inducted and perhaps sent into actual fighting and possible death. It is easy to understand the adolescent's fatalistic attitude and his hostility against authority, his feeling that he might as well enjoy himself while the going is good. If he is pressed for money, he sometimes slips readily into theft, holdups or even more serious crimes. An added complication is that the lad awaiting a call from his Draft Board generally finds that he can only get a routine blind alley job. Anything with a chance for training and advancement is closed to him because employers feel that it is wasteful to train a person who may be taken away after a few months.

Camp life also calls for numerous adjustments. To many young men, going into military service is their first separation from home. Although they had already begun to free themselves from parental control, as is normal in adolescence, they are not emotionally ready for complete emancipation. So they are beset by indecisions and doubts. They are filled with anxiety, not knowing what lies ahead, and they are lonesome because they are cut off from their families and friends and all that is familiar. They are drawn together by their common difficulties and at the same time suspicious of one another and separated by all the religious, social and racial barriers discussed earlier in this chapter. Lonesomeness and need for someone to love may result in furtive recourse to homosexuality or to sexual relations with promiscuous women while away from camp on passes. In either case the young men are having experiences that are poor preparation for wholesome marriage relationships in later life.

As a result of all these new situations, former mild and unrecognized emotional disturbances may burst into definite neuroses. This is why a large number of men have to be discharged as psychoneurotics soon after induction, although they were found physically and psychologically fit at their preinduction examinations.

Even when the new soldiers' difficulties are not manifested in such definite form, the young men are confused and hostile because of the sudden change of status from the increasing independence of civilian life to the rigid discipline and unquestioning obedience of military life. Psychologically, they split the "father figure" into two parts—the bad father and the good father. There is unanimous group hostility toward the sergeant, the bad father figure, and equally unanimous affection and respect for the chaplain, the good father figure. The chaplains of all the faiths—Catholic, Protestant and Jewish—help the boys make the necessary adjustment to their new life by giving advice, comfort and solace, as a good father does. And as the adjustment is made, the sergeant becomes a less threatening figure. It is the expected and accepted thing to "beef" about the sergeant, but he finally becomes a symbol that serves as an outlet for their animosity instead of being a man whom they dislike in any personal way.

The adolescent boy who for some reason is exempt from military service also has problems of adjustment. He may be chagrined or relieved because some defect has set him apart from most of his comrades in this way. In either case, he is likely to take the first job that comes along without much thought of whether or not it is a blind alley one. Despite lack of training he receives what seems to him a large salary—for he is too inexperienced to think in terms of purchasing power and still too young to feel that some of his earnings should be applied to family expenses. Such boys, with money of their own, consider themselves full-fledged adults who no longer need to listen to parental advice. Yet, like the boys at camp, they are not yet ready for complete emancipation. The money they earn is likely to be used for parties, dances, souped-up cars, heavy drinking—participation in whatever gives them an immediate thrill.

Generally these boys, after they have had their fling,

realize that they are getting nowhere, and that they must plan for the future. After their false start they take a more realistic view of life, make some choice about what they want to do, and set about getting training in work that gives promise of advancement and satisfaction.

Girls are also affected by the disruptions of military training and must adjust to the situation of having boys they know in the Services, away from home. Without the companionship of male contemporaries that would be normal for them at this time, some drift into promiscuity, some form attachments with older available men and find themselves involved in relationships, with or without marriage, for which they are not yet ready.

The difficulties faced by the young man in military service —above all, his lonesomeness and need for someone to love— and also faced by the adolescent girl, who cannot reconcile herself to the loss of her special boy friend, often lead young people into marriage before they are mature enough for this step. The inevitable separations of military life at just the time when each of the partners need so urgently to be loved often lead both of them into infidelity. When such couples are finally reunited, they often seem to each other to be strangers, and they realize that the marriage was a mistake. One can readily understand the forces that push so many young people into "war marriages" or "service marriages," and also the forces that make so many of these marriages end in divorce.

As adolescents advance toward adulthood, they encounter many types of situations and many kinds of people. Their reactions and difficulties have been discussed in this chapter. How well they adjust depends on the degree to which they have progressed through the previous phases of their development. If they have progressed in a healthy way, they will have a sense of emotional security and of belonging to their family group, and will have socially constructive attitudes. Given this background, adolescents will feel at home in any situation in which they find themselves. They will be able to make an excellent adjustment to the world in which they live.

CHAPTER NINE

Escape into Illness

SYBIL WAS SEVENTEEN, pretty and charming. She showed promise as a pianist, and everyone in her family, especially her mother, had great hopes for her future. But Sybil had asthma. She could never tell whether she would be able to play at her teacher's recitals or at the country club concerts. Sometimes all went well. Sometimes she had an attack of asthma and couldn't perform.

All through Sybil's childhood her mother had held up to her the great rewards that would come from being a fine pianist. She had coaxed and urged and commanded her to practice. "Now be a good girl," she would say, "and practice, and then Mother'll give you a big hug." Deep inside, Sybil wanted to say, To heck with it, I'd rather play basketball. But she was what we call a good child, well brought up, and it was unthinkable to talk back to Mother. So she took refuge in asthma which, of course, made it impossible to talk.

When I say she took refuge in asthma, I don't for one moment mean that she decided to have it. She didn't know what she was doing, or why. Without understanding at all what was happening, she escaped into illness—in this instance, asthma—from a situation she couldn't cope with.

Constipation, too, is often a form of escape, generally a way of acting against the mother's overstrict bowel training in early childhood.

Alice, a young woman in her twenties, came to me with a history of headaches, constant fatigue and abdominal pains. As

long as she could remember, Alice told me, she had reported
to her mother daily about her bowel movements. Did she or
didn't she? Was her stool normal, or too hard, or too soft?
If her bowels didn't move, mother acted as if a major catastrophe had befallen the household. Medicine, enemas and endless worried discussion were the order of the day. No one had
told Alice that her bowels didn't have to move every single
day. No one had told Alice's mother that in concerning herself so intensely with Alice's bowel movements she was acting
as if her daughter were a child—perpetually a child—at the
toilet training stage. For some reason the mother could not
accept the idea that her daughter had grown up.

Alice fought her mother, defied her—unconsciously—as
best she could. Mother wanted her to have a bowel movement
every day. Well, she just wouldn't. And so she was constipated,
with all the physical results of that condition. She escaped into
this form of illness from a situation she couldn't handle.

The physical difficulties from which these two young
women suffered were manifestations of emotional disturbances.
The effect of these disturbances was, in these instances, clear
cut and crippling. As is to be expected in so complicated a thing
as human reactions, emotional disturbances vary in type and in
intensity and their effects range all the way from harmless
quirks to physical and mental illness.

All of you, I am sure, know something about mental illness. It is discussed today in newspapers, magazines, and books.
It is talked about in lectures and on radio and TV programs.
This is all to the good. The more everyone understands about
mental illness, the more we can do to make these sick people
well and to prevent people from getting sick in this way.

A difficulty arises here that arises in trying to tell the
public about any illness. It is hard to explain things without
frightening people. Take cancer, for example. We all know that

the best way we now have to fight cancer is to tell people about the early signs of this disease, so that they can get help before it is too late. But we also know that there is a risk in doing this. People get worried and frightened; some of them get what we call cancerphobia.

The same thing happens with mental illness. It can be cured, in most cases, if it is treated in time. It can be prevented in most cases if something is done when danger signals appear. Here too, however, there is a risk that people will be frightened and leap at conclusions. The situation is more complicated than in the case of cancer, because the symptoms are less definite, and many normal actions can be falsely construed through ignorance and fear. For example, I might say that moroseness and withdrawal from social contacts are danger signals, but this would not mean that young Johnny is on the verge of a mental breakdown every time he is "low" and wants to be alone in his own room.

Despite these difficulties I believe that parents should be alerted for signals that may indicate that their adolescent children should have medical help. Please note that I say signals that *may* indicate, not that *do* indicate.

To help you understand these signals, how and why they arise, and what they mean, I shall try in this chapter to give you a bird's-eye view of mental and emotional illness, as psychiatrists see it. I do not want you to become "psychiatrists, junior grade," as someone has facetiously labeled laymen who think they know more than they do know about this subject, or indeed than they need to know. I hope, however, that the following discussion will make you less fearful and ill at ease in this field; that it will make it possible for you to help your children when they need help, and will encourage you to seek professional guidance when this is necessary.

The two main types of mental illness are called neuroses

and psychoses. To understand their manifestations, you must know something of how the mind works, and must recall the ground covered, at the beginning of this book, on the formative years.

Every infant and young child has destructive impulses. Gradually, as the child learns to value his mother's tenderness, warmth, and love, he also learns that she disapproves of these impulses. He comes to realize that if he is to retain her love—and, more important, get ever more of it—he must control his destructiveness, and replace it, so to speak, with love. Little by little he recognizes Mother's authority, even when she is not physically with him; he accepts her attitudes and requests, and makes them a part of himself, as if they were his own. Thus he develops a *Conscience* which makes him reluctant—actually, less able—to satisfy his destructive urges.

To avoid conflict, these destructive urges must be "put out of his mind." Where do they go? They are stored away in a part of the mind called the *Unconscious,* or technically the *Id*. This part of the mind harbors all tendencies of the kind which, if gratified, would lead to greater difficulties than the child could cope with. Nothing is forgotten, it is only repressed. This repressed material wants to come out, but the child's conscience does not allow it to do so. The result is restlessness and irritation.

And now what happens? Acting as an agent for compromise between the conscience and the unconscious, is the *Ego*, from the Latin word for "I." Material in the unconscious is constantly seeking expression, and the conscience is constantly warning the ego not to let it be expressed. The ego is caught between the persuasive powers of these two parts of the mind; it must decide what to do. If the conscience is strong enough to influence the ego, a good compromise is effected. If, however, the conscience is so strong that it limits or threatens the ego, the ego will make a poor compromise. Likewise, a poor compromise results whenever the unconscious gains influence over the ego. This is likely to happen when the ego is worn out from constant vigil, from attempting to hold down many undesirable impulses.

All this, I realize, sounds vague. Let us follow it through with something concrete. Let us suppose that Dick, a boy of twelve, has 100 units of ego energy to use for the successful repression of undesirable impulses. He has, let us say, a desire to burn the house, to steal some money from his mother's purse and to masturbate. Each of these drives must be controlled, and he uses 10 units of his ego energy in attempting to control each of them. Now, of course, he has only 70 units left. His ego strength is diminishing. As more situations arise that bring his conscience and his unconscious into conflict and call for further expenditure of ego strength, his ego becomes weaker and weaker. Eventually, Dick might set fire to the house, or steal his mother's money or masturbate. He would not be able to explain why he had done these things, after successfully avoiding them. He would not realize that his ego had finally been weakened to the point where his unconscious impulses could no longer be controlled.

When I speak of 100 units of ego energy and the expenditure of ego strength on a unit basis, I am using an analogy. Like all analogies, it must not be pushed too far or taken too literally. It will, however, serve the purpose of putting unfamiliar material into familiar terms.

Sometimes a compromise is made in the struggle between the conscience and the unconscious. The repressed impulses come out in a disguised way in order to make the ego do the bidding of the unconscious. There is less conflict, because the repressed impulses are satisfied through some form of behavior that is peculiar but socially acceptable. For example, Dick—

our twelve-year-old lad—may overcome his guilt feelings about masturbation by developing what we call a washing ritual—he washes his hands many times every day. What happens to his other two impulses—to burn the house and steal money from his mother's purse?

When we think of fire, we usually also think of water. So Dick satisfies his house-burning impulse by surrounding himself with lots of water. He is eager to play the hose on the lawn at any time—whether the moment is opportune or not. He also takes a bath two or three times a day. By immersing himself in water, he is getting close to mother, through identification with the prebirth intrauterine situation of being surrounded by water; thus he satisfies his need to steal money from Mother's purse—which is really a need to put part of himself, his hand (or phallus), inside his mother's uterus, translated into her purse or "bag."

By frequent baths and washing Dick at one stroke overcomes all three of his impulses. The process of going over to the opposite of the original impulse—fire to water, or masturbation to washing dirty hands—is called *reaction formation*. Dick, through a reaction formation, has produced a *compulsion neurosis*. He is *compelled* to bathe several times a day, for his baths overcome his dangerous impulses to steal, to make a fire or to masturbate. Even if his original impulses fade away and are forgotten, the compulsion neurosis remains. Dick's family may laugh at his strong urge to be immaculately clean, but they might as well accept it.

This is a specific illustration of how a neurosis may develop. Let us put the matter in general terms. A neurosis develops when the balance between conscience and unconscious desires and wishes is disturbed. It is the ego that maintains this balance. It should, ideally, be strong enough to be capable of making all compromises. A good compromise means stability and a minimum of personality disturbance. A poor compromise means a neurosis. A neurosis may be defined as a behavior disorder that arises when repressed desires or impulses, in order to gain satisfaction, manifest themselves in some disguise and an ill-fated compromise results. To understand the particular form that a neurosis takes, we must go back to the formative years and the characteristics of each phase of psychological growth.

The child in the early oral phase, you will recall, is carefree, spontaneous, impulsive and irresponsible. The adolescent—whether boy or girl—who has retained many of these characteristics has a weak conscience. He shows little consideration for others; he cannot stand frustration, cannot think of something and forego its satisfaction. He tends to act out his impulses and to be concerned only with self-satisfaction. His make-up is strongly narcissistic. Such an individual is said to have a neurosis which emotionally reflects his extreme infantilism.

In the late oral phase, you will remember, the young child is afraid of being abandoned and of being unloved. The phase is characterized by anxiety, masochism and pessimism. Most adolescent boys and girls have a tremendous amount of anxiety when they take an examination; they have stage fright when called upon to speak before an audience. Indeed, some degree of anxiety is normal for all of us. If, however, your son or daughter has retained too many of the characteristics of this phase, he may experience anxiety that is based on pessimistic impulses out of all proportion to the specific situation, and on the fear that failure will result in the parents' disapproval and perhaps rejection. He is then apt to develop what is called an *anxiety state*.

Sometimes the boy or girl already feels completely rejected by the parents and knows that the love relationship is totally lacking. Such an adolescent may change his love drives into hostility and aggression, not only against the parents but against the entire environment. Truancy, stealing, vandalism and similar antisocial behavior follow. Collectively such actions are called *chronic aggressive states*.

The anal phase is characterized by the organization of the entire day into various routines, and by a repetition each day of what has been done on the previous one. This phase, you will recall, is the time of habit formation. Ordinarily, as part of our psychological training and growth, we develop discipline and follow routines that are considered normal. In an anally fixated person there may be an element of frustration, and an attempt to overcome the resultant conflict by some form of ritualistic behavior that is directly related to the frustration. I have already given you an example in the young boy who took refuge, as it were, in a washing ritual.

The conscience of a person fixated at the anal phase is usually stronger than that of persons who are not fixated in this way. Such a person's compulsive behavior is an attempt to come to terms with his demanding conscience. Under ordinary circumstances the compulsive neurotic adolescent has no peculiar make-up and shows little anxiety, provided he is able to carry out his ritual. He reveals anxiety only when something interferes with the ritual.

The individual with an *obsessional neurosis* does not express his conflict in acts but in his thoughts. For him, thinking of something is as though it has happened, and the only way he can overcome a "forbidden" thought is to counteract it with another thought—usually the opposite. Such obsessional thoughts take various forms.

William, aged fifteen, was brought to me because he somehow *had* to recite prayers at frequent intervals throughout the day. He became so completely preoccupied with the need for prayer that he actually didn't hear the teacher call upon him to recite in class and could not concentrate on his homework. William's story was soon uncovered. He had been running errands for a retail store. One day, when he was given carfare to deliver a package and return to the store, he walked both ways instead of riding and kept the carfare. Shortly thereafter he developed anxiety and the fear that God would punish him for what he had done. To right himself with God, he had to pray frequently. In fact, every time he thought of having stolen the carfare, he had to say his prayers. He had a religious type of obsessional neurosis.

Another type is the pseudophilosophical. Every time Sam, who was thirteen, saw or heard an airplane overhead, he felt that he had the power to make it crash-land or to redirect its course so that it would crash into another plane. With great restraint, he would control his thoughts and thus avert either calamity. Treatment brought out that his need to destroy airplanes was a redirection of deep inner drives to destroy two of his younger brothers.

Louis, a young man of sixteen, exemplifies the so-called pseudoscientific type of obsessional neurosis. Instead of doing his schoolwork, Louis spent hours memorizing the names, dates and ages of all the presidents of the United States, the makes of all the neighbors' cars and their license numbers; he "had to" identify all the different types of airplanes. Then he would monopolize the dinner conversation by quizzing others at the table about these facts.

There is still a fourth type of obsessional neurosis—that concerned with the body. A boy of twelve, undersized, flat-chested, and with poor muscular development, found it necessary to lift weights many times a day. He also ate voraciously as part of his plan to build up his muscles. He would stand before the mirror, noting the "increase" in the size of his muscles or taking the conventional pose of a muscular athlete. He concentrated on muscle building to the neglect of his studies and of any associations with his peers.

Anxious preoccupation with illness, called *hypochondriasis*, is another neurotic disorder. A minor illness of some part of the body is exaggerated into a very serious illness of the same part. An adolescent boy with a cold on his chest was sure that he had pneumonia, and an adolescent girl with premenstrual cramps developed extreme anxiety and was certain that she had acute appendicitis. Persons suffering from hypochondriasis have constant anxiety about disease and death. They are perfectionists and feel that any slight bodily disorder must be corrected immediately. Basically, hypochondriasis is related to the need to be loved. It is as though such a person feels that Mother will love them only if they are perfect and will withdraw her love at the sign of any flaw. There is ever-present fear that any disorder however minor will not be amenable to correction and will become worse.

In the phallic phase, you will recall, there is tremendous envy and competition. One neurosis associated with fixation at this phase is called *phobia*. It develops as a result of frustration in competition. For example, Phil, an adolescent, feels great hostility against his comrade, Bob, and may actually wish that Bob would die. But Phil has guilt feelings about this wish. He also fears retaliation, for inevitably when we wish for another's death, we fear that we will be paid in kind. A phobia, then, is an unconscious death wish directed against someone else coupled with fear of retaliation. This wish-fear situation is transformed into a phobia of some special kind. The forms that the phobia takes are so numerous that they cannot be listed. A person with a phobia may fear water, or airplanes, or confining spaces, small animals, or large animals, or specific streets, high places, and so on.

In the next stage of psychological growth, the oedipal phase, the young boy develops an attachment to his mother, the young girl develops an attachment to her father, and there is in each case identification with the parent of the same sex. The young child in this phase can generally satisfy his (or her) love drive for the parent of the opposite sex. Later on, in middle adolescence, if there has been fixation at the earlier phase, there may be too great a sense of rivalry with the parent of the same sex and frustration at inability to obtain the love that is needed from the parent of the opposite sex. Some form of *hysteria* may then manifest itself. In other words, hysteria may arise when incestuous tendencies toward the parent of the opposite sex are not successfully repressed. It is invariably based on phantasy and not on memories of actual happenings.

There are two main types of hysteria: mental and physical. One form of *mental hysteria* is what is commonly called sleep walking. The technical term is *somnambulism* from the Latin words *somnus* meaning sleep and *ambulare*, to walk. The sleep walker is in a dream state. If his dreams were analyzed they would show that he had been dreaming of some forbidden sexual relationship and had left his bed to run away from the temptation, or to seek protection and reassurance. For example, a patient of mine, a girl of fifteen, had dreams of being assaulted. She would walk in her sleep to her mother's bed and lie down next to her mother.

You often hear that to awaken a sleepwalker may in some way affect his mind. This is definitely not so. The sleepwalking child should be awakened. Interrupting his dream is no different from interrupting any dream, as you often do when you wake up anyone in the morning.

Daydreaming is another form of mental hysteria, harmless enough when it does not get out of bounds; sometimes, however, it is exaggerated to the point where it takes on the aspects of delirium. Still another form of mental hysteria is *amnesia*, the complete forgetting of a traumatic experience or of a wished-for experience that is filled with frustration. The device of forgetting is protective; in effect, the undesirable experience never occurred. Sometimes, in a protracted state of amnesia, a person forgets not only specific events but everything about his past, including his name. He may establish himself far from home, take another name and carry on a life completely unconnected with his past. Indeed, he is oblivious of his past. This is called a *fugue*, from the Latin word *fuga*, meaning flight. A genuine fugue rarely occurs in adolescence. Although the adolescent often runs away from home, he does so consciously and not because he is suffering from amnesia.

The second main type of hysteria, the physical, is more common in adolescence than the various forms of mental hysteria discussed above. The senses, the motor area, or any other system of the body may be affected in manifestations of *physical hysteria*. The classic example of *hysterical deafness*, with which almost all parents are familiar, is Johnny's failure to hear, actually, when called to do something he doesn't want to do.

Jack, a boy of ten, was brought to me because he claimed that he could not see either to the right or left, and yet he had no difficulty in watching a ball and catching it, whatever its course. Questioning revealed that he slept in the same room with his mother, a widow, and that she permitted her lover to join her in bed on the assumption that the boy was asleep. Jack, however, was wide awake and aware of what was going on. He was caught in the conflict of looking and of not look-ing. His tragic need to repress what was happening was con-verted into *hysterical restriction of the visual field*, so that he actually could not see to right or left. On the basis of this information, Jack was sent to live with his grandmother, and his difficulty promptly disappeared.

In *mutism*, inability to speak, there is a tremendous amount of aggression and hostility, a desire to express it, and also to repress it in order not to alienate the loved one against whom it is directed. The victim takes refuge in not being able to speak.

The following cases illustrate some of the many other forms of physical hysteria. A boy of fifteen came to me complaining of a very severe mineral taste in all the water he drank, no matter what its source. Under treatment he disclosed that he had had a homosexual relationship and had swallowed some of his companion's semen. He had rinsed his mouth, gargled and then taken a drink of water. A few weeks later he noticed for the first time the peculiar taste in all water. Thus he resolved the conflict between wanting to have another homosexual experience and at the same time rejecting the idea.

In the motor sphere, there is often a convulsion that is mistaken for epilepsy. When Agnes, aged nineteen, came to me, she had been having a sort of convulsive seizure once or twice a week during the past eight months. She was fully conscious during the "convulsion," except for a moment just before it subsided. Her parents reported that she had irregular movements of the body, gradually gaining in rapidity, that she threw herself on the bed, then suddenly went limp, and at the end had a strong urge to sleep. Under treatment she remembered her experiences with an Army officer, a close friend of her brother, shortly before the onset of these seizures. She and the young man had gone out together, petted, and gradually indulged more and more in handling each other's genitals. One evening, while doing this, she became frightened, pushed him away and ran upstairs. She never saw him again. About one month later, the seizures began. I was able to explain to her that these

seizures were the result of a conflict between a strong desire
for intercourse and guilt feelings about satisfying that desire.
Through physical hysteria she acted out the sexual experience,
even to the orgasm at the end, followed by sleep.

Margaret's hysteria took a different form. She was brought
to me at the age of fourteen because of complete loss of
appetite. When forced to eat she promptly vomited; she had
lost thirty pounds and all attempts to restore her appetite by
medication had been unsuccessful. This is the story behind her
difficulty: She had been kissed by her uncle, twenty years her
senior, whom she greatly loved and admired, and she had even
had phantasies about how nice it would have been to have a
baby with him. She also recalled that when eight years old she
had believed that a man and woman could "make a baby" by
kissing. So she developed fears that she might have a baby as a
result of her uncle's kissing her, and her rejection of food was
her way of keeping the baby from growing. When the distortions in her thinking were explained to her, she gradually regained her appetite and was able to function normally.

With all these cases in mind, let us sum up the meaning
of hysteria. It is basically a conflict in the adolescent love triangle of father, mother and adolescent. The hysterical individual is very suggestible and self-dramatizing; he is seeking
sympathy, tenderness and love. The manifestation of hysteria
is a defense against forbidden impulses, or a disguise for the
real drive that is seeking satisfaction. When the basis of the
hysterical manifestation is uncovered, and the adolescent is
given an understanding of the conflict that the hysteria is trying to resolve, the hysterical disorder almost always clears up.

The mental disorders we have discussed thus far are
neuroses of various kinds. They develop, as I have explained,
when the balance between conscience, ego and unconscious
is disturbed. The second of the two main types of mental illness,

you will recall, are the psychoses. These also develop when the three elements of the mind are out of balance. There is, however, a difference in the way in which the balance is disturbed. In a neurosis, whatever its form, the conscience is sufficiently strong to control the ego and prevent it from letting the unconscious bring out the impulses that are lodged there. The unconscious then disguises its impulses and they manifest themselves in the various forms of neurosis I have described and illustrated. The converse process takes place in a psychosis. It is the unconscious that is the stronger and that is able to overpower the ego. Thus it is able to bring up its impulses *directly*, instead of having to *disguise* them.

The most common form of psychosis is *schizophrenia*, from the two Greek words meaning split or cleavage and mind. Although schizophrenia is rare in adolescence it does occur, and must be considered here to make our survey complete. A word first about childhood schizophrenia. It is now recognized that there is some constitutional disorder that produces schizophrenia in early childhood. It is not yet clearly understood what it is. Schizophrenia arising in adolescence, on the other hand, generally develops in a person who as a child was overprotected and overindulged by his parents. His history usually reveals that when any difficulty arose the parent or some other adult promptly took over, instead of letting the child handle it. Then, when this child, grown older, is faced with the adjustments of adolescence—school and home situations, and physical, endocrine and sexual changes—he cannot cope with the problems that arise. He escapes into phantasy, and accepts phantasy in place of the reality he cannot handle. He gives up the world around him and in its place develops a world of his own.

It may be that the pattern of early overprotection arose from failure of the child to function properly and the natural

urge of the parents to "cover up" for him and for themselves—
that is, not to acknowledge that there was anything wrong.
Thus the childhood history generally uncovered in adolescent
schizophrenia may possibly indicate some unrecognized psychological difficulty in childhood. It goes without saying that
not all overindulged and overprotected children develop schizophrenia in adolescence. There are many unknown factors in
the situation. Moreover, it should be noted, this childhood
pattern is not invariably found and not all schizophrenia can
be explained in this way.

The unconscious expresses itself directly in schizophrenia,
and its expressions take many forms. People who are dead
are considered alive; God and Jesus actually exist in the flesh
today; everything is timeless; the individual can transport himself anywhere (like the little child on a magic carpet), or can
transform himself into anything—an animal, a tree, a house.
The schizophrenic individual can carry on conversations with
God, and they are to him not imaginary but real. He can con-
vert his body into a receiving or transmitting station, can send
out electrical charges that can destroy the entire world, and so
on.

In one form of schizophrenia called *paranoia*, the processes
of distortion are quite different. The paranoid cannot accept
impulses from his unconscious as originating within himself,
and so he distorts the impulse and believes that it comes from
the environment. Basically, he is hostile toward the environment and wants to destroy it. He claims, however, that the
reverse is true—that the environment is hostile to him and
wants to destroy him. He rationalizes this by believing that the
hostility is caused by his ability and superiority over others,
and he uses a sort of illogical logic that makes it difficult to
break down his reasoning.

Larry, aged fourteen, told me that in his tenth year certain boys at school threw spitballs at him. He was convinced that they did this because he was a brilliant student and superior to them in every way. From that time until he came to me, he kept a little book with the names and addresses of all the individuals who had "done anything" to him, and he planned to keep the list up-to-date. At some future time, he said, when these people least suspected harm, he would kill them.

Fortunately, Larry's type of mental disorder, schizophrenia of the paranoid type, is extremely rare in adolescence.

One more form of psychosis should be noted here— *depression.* The situations that arise in adolescence sometimes seem made to order to produce depression—competition and rivalry for friends, for scholastic and athletic honors and so on. The normal girl and boy take these things in stride. The psychotic may go into a depression. There is self-examination and self-criticism, self-blame and hopelessness. And sometimes this hopelessness is changed into vindictiveness.

I spoke at the beginning of this chapter of a young woman who had asthma and another who had constipation as the result of emotional disturbances. These are *psychosomatic* disturbances. The word comes from the Greek *psyche* and *soma,* meaning mind and body. We hear a great deal today about psychosomatic illness, an indication of a growing awareness that mind and body are one unified whole. Actually, adolescents rarely have psychosomatic disorders, for the very simple reason that there has not yet been time for physiological effects of the emotional disturbances to become chronic. This statement brings us squarely to a consideration of *prevention,* the basic purpose I have in mind in writing this chapter.

There are, as you certainly realize, various degrees and kinds of neuroses. Some are harmless quirks, such as having to throw salt over your shoulder to avoid bad luck, and some are sufficiently serious to interfere with successful and happy living.

It is these that must have attention, so that they can be corrected before they become more serious. Although an unresolved neurosis never predisposes a person to psychosis, it can be so crippling that it completely overwhelms an affected boy or girl.

Evidence of behavior such as I have described in this chapter should be considered a danger signal, an indication of the possibility of mental illness. Do something about it. If your boy gets into a washing ritual, as I have described, don't laugh at him or try to jolly him out of it. Talk with him and try to find out why he is acting in this way. Sometimes it is possible to talk things out. Sometimes, however, your boy will not talk, or, what is more likely, simply cannot talk things out. This is the time to get professional help. In most cases, your family physician can deal with the trouble.

Present-day medical education includes training in handling mental and emotional illnesses as well as clear-cut physical disorders. Your family doctor will know when more specialized treatment by a psychiatrist is needed, just as he knows when care by a surgeon or other specialist is needed. One suggestion is in order here. If you see in your young son or daughter one or another of the danger signals I have described, first go to your doctor yourself and talk things over before sending your child to him. In this way he will get a more complete picture of the situation.

I have said that schizophrenia is comparatively rare in adolescence. You should, however, be alert for any sudden changes in personality, in habits, mode of living or thinking, and seek help at once. Neuroses, on the other hand, occur frequently. Use common sense in recognizing them and dealing with them, just as you use common sense in recognizing and dealing with minor physical ills. In other words, be alert to the possibility of something serious but do not be overanxious or frightened.

Keep in mind that as the teen-ager becomes more adjusted to the environment of adulthood and more confident of his own capacities, many neuroses disappear or become so slight that they do not interfere with normal functioning.

CHAPTER TEN

Escape into Delinquency

MR. A., A WEALTHY BUSINESSMAN, came to me in great distress because his son Terry had stolen his watch. Why did Terry do it, Mr. A. asked over and over again. He had an adequate allowance and could have bought a watch for himself. If he didn't want to spend his own money, his parents would gladly have given him a watch.

"But didn't you know he wanted one?" I queried. "Boys aren't usually bashful about asking for things."

"Well—well—" Mr. A.'s decisive business-executive voice faltered. "Fact is, we don't have much time to talk with Terry. We're on the go a lot. You know how it is. . . ."

Mr. A. had no intention of reporting this theft to the police. He was focused on the main issue, the cause. I purposely leave this story unfinished and pass to another one.

I first saw Jack when he was in the hospital with severe burns. He was nine, the oldest of seven children. His mother went out to work by the day and the father "deserted now and then," as the social workers put it. The family managed as best they could in a tumbledown shanty on the outskirts of Flatbush. Jack had never had a complete outfit of clothes or a square meal in his life. What little there was to eat went first to the baby, then to the next in age and so on. Little was left for the oldest—little food and what is more important little love or attention from the mother. Jack had set fire to the house and had been rescued along with his brothers and sisters. He was in a bad spot. The burns that had landed him in the hospital were the least of his difficulties. Later he would face arson charges as a juvenile delinquent.

Here, then, are two antisocial acts—stealing and arson. Why were they committed? One lad was wealthy, the other poverty-stricken. One lived on New York's fashionable Park Avenue, the other in a substandard slum. One could gratify his every whim and desire. The other had nothing and no chance of even getting enough of such fundamental things as food and clothing, let alone toys and movies. These two boys, however, had one thing in common—lack of love and understanding in their homes. They were rejected by their parents.

Here then is the key to delinquency. Technically, it is a legal term. An adolescent is delinquent when his behavior brings him into conflict with the law, when he does something that the law calls a delinquent act. It may be a minor offense or a serious crime.

Legally Terry, who stole his father's watch, is not a juvenile delinquent because his father did not report his theft to the police. Jack, who set fire to his mother's shack, is a juvenile delinquent because the police caught him. We need not be concerned, however, with these technicalities. I want to focus on the antisocial act, whatever its legal outcome, and on its basic causes.

We are led astray by the fact that the adolescent who tangles with the law and ends up in a reformatory is usually a boy or girl who has had an impoverished childhood in a slum environment. It is easy to conclude that poverty and lack of economic opportunities are the basic causes of juvenile delinquency. But, as we have seen in the two cases I have cited, the wealthy lad as well as the poor one does antisocial things. These cases can be multiplied many hundred times.

There is one common denominator in all of them, however much they differ in other ways. The adolescent delinquent has a background—a home environment—in which no one loves him or pays any attention to him or tries to understand him. I have described in the previous chapter how some adolescents escape from difficulties which they cannot overcome by taking refuge in mental illness. Sometimes their escape takes a different and more aggressive form. They become delinquents.

The cause of delinquency is not poverty, as is too often thought. It is not subnormal housing, or lack of recreational facilities and educational opportunities, or suggestions and stimulation by comic books, movies and radio. All these things may give direction and form to antisocial acts, but they are not in themselves—singly or in combination—responsible for the acts.

The basic and primary cause of delinquency is emotional insecurity. When there is any disturbance in the wholesome, loving and understanding relationship between the child and his parents, or between the parents themselves, then he inevitably feels emotionally insecure. He is perhaps rejected by the parents, or by one of them; in the latter instance, rejection by the mother has the more disastrous effects. He is perhaps overindulged by the parents, or by one of them; here too, the attitude of the mother is the more serious. He has perhaps grown up in an atmosphere of strife and tension caused by unsatisfactory marital relations between the parents. Whatever the situation, if it results in the child's striving unsuccessfully for love and having a sense of emotional insecurity, he may escape into delinquency.

Since delinquency is frequently associated with truancy, I want to show you how truancy begins. During the first years of life, as you know, the child has been number one in his own little world, the center of his mother's attention. At the age of five or six, he enters a different world, that of school. With ten, twenty or sometimes fifty other children, he must compete for the love and attention of the teacher, who is the mother substitute in this new world. He may set himself to doing well with his lessons, and thus gain self-satisfaction and praise from both mother and teacher. His exercise book is studded with stars, he is proud of his success and has a sense of belonging and of being loved. The emotional security he had at home as a small child has carried over into this larger world, and all is well.

But what if for some reason he does not take this course? What if he cannot, or will not, satisfy his need for attention by excelling and winning the teacher's praise? There are other ways of gaining attention. Let us see what happens to Mike, who follows these other ways.

Mike wanders around the room, he is reprimanded and made to sit down. He taps with his foot or pencil, spills the ink, crushes a piece of chalk on the floor, or throws chalk or spitballs at the other pupils. Each misdeed results in a scolding by the teacher and also, of course, in attention from her—which is just what he wants. Perhaps the teacher puts Mike in a corner with his face to the wall. He peeks around, sticks out his tongue or thumbs his nose, and his antics are rewarded by giggles and laughter from his classmates. So he gets their attention, too. Finally the teacher can no longer put up with his pranks and sends him out of the room to the Principal's office. Now Mike has lost his "audience." He has been rejected by the teacher and is no longer part of her "family." He feels irritated and bitter, and he is angry with her. Small wonder that in this mood he decides to stay away from school. He hoodwinks his mother by leaving home each morning as though going to school, but he never gets there. Mike has become a truant.

Roaming the streets he meets up with other boys who are also truants, and they band together into a gang. Each member feels guilty and furtive and inadequate by himself, but as part of a group he feels strong and able to express his hostility. Mike and the other boys in his gang hold up other children and take things from them—pennies and nickels, baseball bats, balls, and even, if they are daring, bicycles and possessions of similar worth. Each member of the gang carries a small pocketknife, and in their holdups the knives are open, with the blade threateningly in view. Soon, emboldened by success, the gang begins to steal fruit from the corner fruitstand and small objects from the five-and-ten-cent store and the drugstore. On the surface, it appears that the boys are stealing for the thrill and adventure, but underneath and unconsciously they are trying to overcome their emotional insecurity by taking away other males' possessions.

In the universal language of symbols, any sharp-pointed object, such as a knife, a closed umbrella, the prow of a ship, a sword, a bayonet, represents the penis. Any hollow tube through which small objects can be shot—a gun, a cannon, a garden hose—is also considered as a symbol of the penis. In psychiatric treatment, this symbolism shows up clearly in patients' dreams. Objects such as those I have listed are commonly used by the dreamer as disguises for the penis. The knives that the boys use are phallic symbols. By threatening people with knives they are really symbolically threatening rivals with mutilation—that is, with castration.

Mike and his fellow truants grow older and are now adolescents. They have changed their little knives for big knives and switchblades, and they continue their stealing. There is a definite thrill in beating the law—for authority stands for the father and these boys have a great need to overcome the father. You will recall the rivalry between father and adolescent boy, described in the first part of this book. In the maladjusted adolescent who takes refuge in delinquency it becomes destructive. It is a desire to annihilate not only the father but all men.

Rivalry and hostility toward all men is the keynote of

these boys' activities. The gangs formed on the basis of truancy in childhood have developed into openly aggressive gangs that engage in "warfare," one street or other grouping against another, and in place of knives they use guns.

Consider, for a moment, how one might describe a gun— a long slender barrel through which small "pellets" are ejected (ejaculated)—and you will see how a gun is an even more direct phallic symbol than a knife. So the gangs of adolescent delinquents, carrying out ever more serious antisocial acts, are activated—unconsciously, remember—by a need to destroy their peers and all competition and to be the victors.

Mike, in addition to having a gun, now probably has a girl (the gun moll) whom he idolizes and protects. She is his property and he defends her against any other boy who tries to take her away. Mike loves his girl but rarely has a sexual relationship with her, for she stands for the mother. Thus he has regained, as it were, what he lost when he first went to school— the sole love and attention of his mother or teacher.

I have been describing, in the story of Mike, what happens when a boy cannot adjust to school life after being number one in his mother's eyes at home. The boy who has a feeling of having been rejected at home during his preschool years may also find it difficult to adjust. Throughout his formative years he has been uncertain of his mother's love. Time and again she has given him some attention only to withdraw it. Even if he succeeds in winning the love and attention of the teacher, his previous experience of rejection makes him feel that sooner or later she too will abandon him. So he too may take the truancy road that may lead to adolescent delinquency.

At the beginning of this chapter I said that emotional insecurity is the basic cause of delinquency. Sometimes this insecurity does not manifest itself in the early school years but in the early or mid-adolescent period. Sidney was not a small-boy truant. He was the victim in mid-adolescence of constant quarrels at home and a total lack of the relationship with his father that is so necessary for normal development. His need to be loved, his need for approval made him turn to an older boy for the attention he could not get at home. He stole to give this boy gifts, or perhaps he stole because the other boy ordered him to do so. He also permitted the older boy to have a homosexual relation with him. Such perversion is very likely to continue throughout adolescence and even during adulthood.

It would seem at first glance that a teen-ager who steals does so under the necessity of poverty, to obtain something his parents cannot buy for him or he cannot buy for himself. Closer examination shows that stealing in adolescence knows no economic boundaries. Most boys, both poor and wealthy, do not steal, and conversely some boys, whether they are poor or wealthy, do steal. We have the key to this riddle in the basic cause of delinquency—emotional insecurity. The lad who steals lacks something that has nothing to do with money. He lacks parental love and a sense of belonging. He may steal to prove his superiority over his father, to give his mother what his father is unable or unwilling to give her, thus displacing him, or at least gaining the mother's attention. And, as I have already pointed out, he steals to take away other men's possessions, thus "proving" his superiority over them.

Often the adolescent's delinquent actions are distorted reflections of what he sees at home, of the way his parents behave. In his desire to be grown-up and to emulate them, he crosses the line that separates what is socially acceptable in adult life and what is delinquent in an adolescent.

Phil, who was brought to me by his father, was sixteen and at high school. He had begun to play cards some years before, had learned to play a good game of poker and had gradually joined in games with older men, playing for high stakes. He won a great deal of money and then began to gamble in other ways. He acted as a "bookmaker" at high school, taking bets on baseball, football and basketball games. He got in with a fast set and took less and less interest in his school work. When he was about to be flunked out, his father for the first time took notice of how his son was spending his time.

"Why does he have to gamble," the father asked. "It's not as if he needed the money. I'd buy him anything he asked for."

Phil didn't need the money, but he needed something far more valuable and harder to get, and he needed it desperately. I learned, during the course of treatment, that the boy, an only child, had never had a normal home life. His father, coming home from business, would kick off his shoes and settle down to checking the afternoon's horse races on which he had placed many bets. For an hour he was not to be disturbed, and he had no time for Phil. At dinner time, both parents talked exclusively about horses, winnings, and bets for the following day. Phil's doings were of no concern to them. Invariably, after dinner, the parents went to their bedroom for a nap and then out for an evening of cards. They rarely came home until the small hours. Excluded from his parents' lives, it was no wonder that Phil tried to do as they did by copying their interests and their mode of living.

Similarly, another lad of sixteen was brought to me because he was drinking heavily and getting into difficulties. He had been reared in an environment of parties and heavy drinking, of loose talk, and tales of extramarital affairs. His parents had "no time" for him. It is easy to understand why he tried to emulate them and in this way tried to feel grown up. He began to drink heavily just as his parents and their friends did, and he had his share of women, too.

Thus cheating, drinking, conniving and gambling are often reflections of similar actions on the part of the adolescent's parents.

Gambling, especially, has deep psychological implications for the adolescent. It is a way of assuaging his turmoil and conflicts about his own worth and about whether he is loved. If he wins, he feels as good as or better than other boys. He is getting their belongings, and he is smug in his omnipotence. Lady Luck is at his side, invoking some magic formula for his benefit. Luck is the mother figure, protecting him just as his mother protected him as a baby, giving him not only his share but more than his share. He is chosen by Luck (Mother) in preference to all other "men." In gambling the lad unconsciously tests his environment, seeks to assure himself that he is loved. By winning he proves to himself that he is superior to other men. Winning or losing, the adolescent gets a thrill out of gambling because through his close association with other men he satisfies his homosexual urge.

The problem of addiction to narcotics among adolescents is acute today. Like other forms of delinquency, addiction is rooted in personality difficulties. It is found that, with striking uniformity, young addicts are fixated at the oral phase, at which—you will recall—the infant is cared for and cherished without putting forth any effort, receives everything he needs and gives nothing in return and has no responsibilities whatsoever. The teen-age addict, like the infant, is nonaggressive, easily manipulated, naive. Unconsciously as though by magic and phantasy he is seeking to recapture the comfortable, protected, and loving environment of his lost infancy. With such traits he often drifts into addiction quite innocently.

What happened to Ted is typical. He was a pleasant, quiet boy of fourteen, who looked a good deal older than his years. He was unpopular at school—inept in athletics and somewhat sluggish scholastically. Ted began to hang around at the corner saloon, listening to the man-talk, taking a beer when it was offered to him, trying vicariously to be someone in this grown-up world. Soon a man asked whether he wanted to earn a few bucks for delivering a small package to a nearby address. He gladly did the errand, and then another and still another, pocketing the relatively high pay for the easy tasks. Curiosity soon got the better of Ted and he discovered that he was delivering narcotics. The man who was sending him on his errands began to fill his ears with stories of how happy he would feel if he tried the powder, and gave him some "free samples." To prove to himself that he was not afraid, and because he was by nature naive and trusting—like a little child— Ted tried out the drug. The result was all that could be wished for. Gone were Ted's fears and conflicts, his feelings of inadequacy. In the dream state induced by the drug, Ted was able blissfully to become again a carefree, irresponsible infant surrounded by unstinting love and attention.

Boys like Ted are fixated at the oral phase of their development, as I have pointed out, and they are ill-equipped to face the problems that confront them in their teens. At this age boys are normally meeting stiff competition from their peers, they are trying to be independent and are expected to make all kinds of decisions for themselves. The boys who become victims of drug addiction cannot meet these challenges.

At school, despite normal or better than normal IQs, they have not been able to absorb instruction either in intellectual fields or in manual skills. They are inept, and they have no definite plans for the future.

The typical home situation reveals a weak father of little

ability or no father, and a domineering mother who has been overprotective during the boy's formative years and is now harshly critical of his lack of ability. You will recall that in the crucial period of middle adolescence, the boy should be able to identify with a strong and admirable father figure, and should develop a relationship with his mother that encourages him gradually to assume the role of a male. In a home such as I have described here, these normal processes are thwarted. The mother is always at hand to help the boy, and she is also critical, because whatever he attempts to do is not successfully carried out. As a result, the boy feels dependent and rejected. He has no opportunity to develop relationships with his parents that will help him grow and mature.

Such boys are emotionally insecure, they have no sense of belonging, and an inordinate urge for approval of any kind, from any source. In an effort to gain from their peers the acceptance they are deprived of at home and at school, they accept a dare and "take a shot." Miraculously, they now have all that was formerly lacking—a sense of belonging, a feeling of being important, approval and love. To maintain this aura of well-being, they want more shots. But the samples that they have received free are no longer available. The problem of how to obtain shots is solved by pilfering or stealing, or by participating in homosexual relations in the passive role for a fee, which they use to buy the drug.

Boys who are drug addicts and who attempt heterosexual relations do not seem to enjoy them; they are disturbed and in conflict about the experience. Actually, they do not want a man-woman relationship, but a mother-son relationship characteristic of the one-year-old child. The drug addict generally loses the desire for adult sexual relations and becomes impotent. Thus he regains the magic dream state of infancy and is released from his conflict over his "Oedipus situation." Perhaps he drifts toward homosexuality as a step down on the ladder of emotional development to the homosexual level of early adolescence, as a way of seeking satisfaction with a minimum of conflict. When addicts have a choice between having a girl or a shot, they prefer the shot, and if they are deprived of the drug for a period of time they return to frequent masturbation.

The effect of various narcotics is not identical, and a distinction must therefore be made between smoking marijuana (reefers) and taking heroin or cocaine. The former is not, strictly speaking, addiction since it does not create the craving that characterizes the use of heroin. The boy who smokes reefers feels uninhibited and carefree; he is over excitable, overtalkative and "high." He behaves in much the same way as the boy who is drunk from alcohol. In this state he can get into all kinds of trouble, just like the boy who drinks heavily. In general, boys who smoke reefers finally recognize that they are doing something abnormal and give it up. In saying this, I am not minimizing the seriousness of the vice, for the reefer smoker, because his judgment is warped, is apt to get into serious scrapes and commit delinquent acts.

Heroin is the true addiction drug, for it produces extreme craving that makes it well-nigh impossible to stop using it. Its effects are quite different from the effects of reefers. The boy who takes heroin feels placid and drowsy. He is contented and satisfied with life, unperturbed and at ease. Boys under the influence of heroin are not a problem to their teachers. Unlike other delinquents, the narcotic addict is not aggressive. He accepts orders, avoids arguments, does not talk back or get into fights. He is usually quiet and controlled. Thus teachers do not detect narcotic users in the classroom; they are often astonished when informed that their quiet tractable pupil is a narcotic addict.

What produces the extreme craving that is the mark of

addiction? Originally, the boy comes back for more to retain his feeling of satisfaction. Then, during a period of abstinence, either in an attempt to give up his newly acquired habit or because he cannot get hold of the stuff, he develops various physical symptoms, ranging from restlessness, mild anxiety and loss of appetite to profuse sweating, watering of the eyes, profuse discharge of mucus from the nose, diarrhea and abdominal cramps. It has been claimed that the addict returns to the drug to avoid these severe physical discomforts. This view seems to be refuted by the fact that those who have had institutional care and no longer have the physical symptoms also tend to return to the habit. Hence it is logical to conclude that the basis for the craving is immature psychological make-up and social maladjustment, the lure of replacing the frustrations of reality with the satisfactions of phantasy.

Not all boys who have used narcotics succumb to this craving and become addicts. Some are able to conquer their desire for the drug. Those who continue to use it, however, seem to be doomed for life. Because of their weak ego, psychological contact with them is difficult, and with no change in their basic psychology they continue to seek phantasy satisfaction. Their need for group approval remains unchanged, and is satisfied through addiction either in the environment in which they began to take the drug, or in a different environment.

In theory, the problem could be solved by making the drug inaccessible through legal control, but the practical difficulties of completely controlling distribution have thus far been insurmountable.

At the opening of this chapter I pointed out that an adolescent is legally delinquent only when his behavior brings him in conflict with the law. The so-called pranks of college boys rarely lead to arrest and punishment under the law, and therefore they are not technically delinquent acts. Moreover, we are generally indulgent about what college boys do, shrugging off their pranks as part of a phase that will soon be outgrown. Sometimes these pranks become serious. In essence, college boys' stealing, gambling, cheating and sex escapades are no different, psychologically speaking, from similar delinquent acts of other boys. Only the setting is different.

It is quite the thing for a college boy to decorate his room with stolen street and subway signs, and even lampposts, and to display stolen hotel towels. Proprietors of stores close to a college campus say that anything detachable will be lifted and carried away by the students as "a souvenir." All this stealing is, of course, done for the thrill, but there are also implications of sexual satisfaction in such acts, in that the young men are taking away the possessions of other men and thereby increasing their own potency.

Gambling at poker, gin rummy, or bridge is a popular extracurricular activity. I have already discussed the psychological implications of gambling. They are the same, whether the game for stakes that are too high is played in a college dormitory or a slum pool parlor. Often college boys, pushing luck too far, lose the money given them by their parents for everyday living expenses and are unable to explain to Dad why they are running short. The easy way out is to try to recoup their losses by stealing some other boy's jewelry or books and selling them. So gambling may lead to stealing.

Sometimes stealing is not based on necessity but is a form of revenge. A college boy told me that after a particularly acrimonious argument with a fellow student he stole a number of articles from different rooms in the dormitory and planted them in his "enemy's room." When they were discovered, his enemy was expelled, and thus he won the argument.

The basis of stealing may be even more intricate, as Donald's story shows. Donald was brought to me by his bewildered parents toward the end of his freshman year at college after he had been expelled for stealing. He had made good marks and seemed all set for success as a student. He did not himself know why he stole fellow students' sweaters and tennis rackets, books and fountain pens, and he acknowledged that he had an adequate allowance and did not need any of these things. Strangely enough, Donald stole because he was homesick. Overindulged in childhood by doting parents, he had been unable to adjust to the social life of college, despite the fact that he did well enough scholastically. He felt isolated and friendless, rejected and forlorn. Unconsciously he wanted to get back to the safe and snug harbor of home. And so he sabotaged his college career by stealing; his urge to regain the security of the home environment was so great that he really unconsciously expelled himself.

We read every now and then of panty raids at coeducational colleges. The men on campus by means of ropes, human ladders, wall climbing, and scurrying across roofs and fire escapes somehow gain admittance to the girls' dormitories. The girls egg the boys on, and there is much laughter and high erotic feeling. The boys flout the authority of campus police, college officers, house mothers, and finally one of them gets into a girl's room. She surrenders her panties with a great show of resistance, and there is a lot of gay rolling on the bed and the floor, laughter and erotic thrills. The boy finally emerges, proudly displaying his trophy.

The panty raid has a deep inner meaning. Some hundred or more "men" take part in the raid. Any one of them singly would not have the prowess to carry matters through, but as a group they are strong enough to flout authority and act out the phantasy of seduction and rape. The girls, too, by teasing the men and urging them on, by putting on a show of resistance are playing their part in this phantasy.

Another form of delinquency that is rife at college is cheating. It takes many forms. When term papers have to be written and research projects have to be carried through, it is an easy matter to take and copy a paper written by some upper classman or former student, conveniently kept on file in a fraternity, or to get an old paper from some acquiescent upper classman. At examinations, all sorts of ingenious devices are employed—crib notes, books on the floor or adjacent seats, reading over the shoulder of some obliging fellow student or even taking the examination by proxy. Occasionally, the professor's office is entered by force and the examination questions are stolen in advance. The lad who does this often sells the questions to others as well as using them himself in preparing for the examination.

The college boy who cheats generally rationalizes his actions. "It's a crappy course," he says. "The prof is lousy—the subject is dull—I'm too busy with outside things and didn't have time to study." The real reason why he cheats, however, is that he feels inadequate, he fears failure and has a great need for approval from his teachers and parents. He does not realize that cheating indicates poor inner control, little inner discipline, a false concept of success and an inert conscience. Cheating establishes a way of living that may prove troublesome, if not disastrous, later in life.

It is sometimes said that adolescents with lower than average mentality tend to become delinquents and criminals. Fortunately it is possible to train individuals of limited mental capacity so that they can function in society and carry on happy useful lives. Sometimes, however, adolescents of this type are confused and in conflict because they are unable to keep up with other boys of normal intelligence and the same age. They then can readily become the pawns of boys who direct their activities into delinquent channels. Since they generally do not understand what is going on, and have less resourcefulness and guile than their more capable companions, they are usually the ones who are caught, brought to trial and punished. Tragically, they are unable to profit from experience because of their limited mentality, and generally, after being liberated from a correctional institution, they are again implicated in some criminal activity.

Up to this point I have discussed the adolescent boy who escapes into delinquency. What of the delinquent girl? Unlike the boy, her delinquency rarely begins with early truancy and gang formations. It generally starts at the onset of menses and manifests itself in some form of sexual misbehavior.

You will recall that a young girl passes through a phase of strong love for her father and of conflict because that love cannot, of course, be completely satisfied. Normally she is satisfied with some show of affection from her father and is able to control her sexual drive. Her incest taboo is sufficiently great to protect her. When she does not get any affection from her father, or when there is no father—it matters not why he is absent—then events may not move so smoothly. The girl may try to satisfy this love for her father by seeking out some other older man. Here the incest taboo does not protect her. It is an almost inevitable step from petting and caressing to sexual indulgence. And another step from sexual intercourse with this man to indulgence with another man and still another. The sexual act itself has become a necessity, although the "chain reaction" that started it was itself started by a drive that is a normal part of growing up. Studies of sexual delinquency show that girls who have been orphaned in childhood or who have grown up with the father absent are more likely than other girls to get into this kind of trouble.

Disharmony between the parents and their infidelity sometimes drive a girl into sexual delinquency. Wanting, as is normal, a love relationship with the father and hearing of his affairs with other women, she identifies herself with these women and feels, unconsciously, that if she is promiscuous like them her father will turn his attentions to her. Somewhat similarly, when the adolescent girl learns of her mother's infidelity she may identify with her and seek the same pleasures.

A number of other situations can also lead to sexual delinquency. Patricia, called Pat, wanted to be a man; she rejected her own femaleness and had a strong drive for maleness. This drive was satisfied only by sexual promiscuity. Every time she had sexual relations she "acquired" the penis of her partner, and by incorporation it became her penis. Through numerous sexual experiences with many men she had, as it were, many penises and was now more masculine than any one man. Her promiscuity also helped her reject her own femaleness, by the misuse and abuse of her genitals. Pat had no desire to be loved. Indeed she was hostile toward each of her male partners and wanted only to weaken him by "taking away" his penis. Because she had not been born a boy, Pat's basic drive was hostility toward her mother.

The desire for dates and the need to be popular sometimes leads young girls into sexual delinquency. They feel that they cannot be left out, that they must go along with the "other girls," and the fact that they conform to the customs of their peers eases their conscience and allays their sense of guilt. The tragedy of rape during the early adolescent period may also lead to promiscuity. Such girls feel besmirched and abandon any hope of establishing a love relationship with any one man and of getting married. And so they feel that they might as well enjoy what they can have, a life of prostitution.

In addition to the most prevalent form of delinquency in adolescent girls which I have been discussing, mention should be made of shoplifting and drug addiction. The former is the outstanding type of theft in the adolescent girl. Basically, she is seeking to obtain the unobtainable, that is, male genitals. And she satisfies this drive by taking possessions from a store—out-witting the owners and flouting the law.

Drug addiction is not as prevalent in girls as in boys, but it does exist to the extent of being a serious problem. The girl who becomes a drug addict, like the boy victim, is fixated at the oral phase of development, but unlike the boy, who wishes to remain a child, the girl has a strong urge to become a mature woman. She is thwarted in this desire because she has been stunted psychologically.

During the crucial middle adolescent period, her father has rejected her or has been openly hostile to her, and mother and daughter have been constantly at odds, since the girl has struggled against the mother's domination. This girl has a strong sexual urge and craves attention, affection and love from men, but she is in conflict about performing the sex act and she has a great need to lessen her guilt about it. Thus the stage is set, psychologically speaking, for her becoming a victim of addiction through exposure to a narcotic drug.

This usually comes about through a sexual partner who is a drug addict or a drug peddler. To overcome her reluctance, which amounts to an inability to participate, he prods her into taking some stuff. It has the desired effect. Her inhibitions are gone, and she is now a willing partner. It is then only a matter of a few more "inducements" until she begins to accept the sat-isfaction of sexual relations and overcomes her inner sexual conflicts. To obtain supplies, she is ready to work as a prostitute, either in a house or independently. And so drug addiction and prostitution go hand in hand.

These girls have good social awareness and usually better than normal intelligence. They express themselves well and act grown-up. They seem to attach themselves to wealthy addicts with whom they have a close relationship, not only sexually but socially. Because of the ease with which they are able to obtain supplies, either through such a relationship or through prostitution, and because their sexual urge is satisfied through the influence of the drug, they are most inaccessible to treatment.

In closing the discussion of delinquency, I want to emphasize that only a small percentage of adolescents—about 5 per cent—are delinquent. The vast majority pass unscathed through the difficulties and adjustments of psychological development. Public attention has focused so sharply on so-called juvenile delinquency that we are apt to think that the problem is quantitively greater than it is.

Because curiosity about the unknown adult world and the drive for independence are natural in adolescence, there will inevitably be some misbehavior. It should be accepted and understood for what it is, and should not be confused with the serious antisocial acts that add up to delinquency. I hope that I have succeeded in showing you that when adolescents have a sense of emotional security, a feeling of being loved and of "belonging," they will not cross the line that divides socially acceptable misbehavior from delinquency. When this line is crossed, we must try to understand why. Our concern must not be with punishment but with removing the conditions that led to delinquency. We must help the adolescent understand himself and why he has done forbidden things. He will then be able to overcome his anger and rebellion, his frustration and despair in less destructive ways.

Sometimes, strangely enough, delinquency solves itself. The man who has been a juvenile delinquent, and who has continued to be a criminal long after he was an adult in years, though not in other ways, sometimes turns over a new leaf in his mid-thirties. Perhaps he has by then less physical stamina and agility—qualities that are necessary attributes for a criminal life. Perhaps he has come to realize, through repeated prison terms or through religious or other influences, that "crime does not pay." Perhaps some psychological forces that are not entirely clear to us are at work. Whatever the reason, criminologists tell us that a change may take place in the mid- or late thirties. The former criminal, who started out as a juvenile delinquent, learns a trade, applies himself, and does well at his job; he settles down to respectable family life; he may become a fervent crusader against crime. If such a change does not occur at this time, criminologists say, it probably will not occur at all.

Can we take this chance, trust to luck, and hope that delinquency will solve itself, as it sometimes does? Or shall we try to prevent juvenile delinquency, or—failing that—give the adolescent the attention and guidance he so much needs as speedily as possible, in the hope of making him a worthwhile and happily functioning member of society?

I have emphasized that delinquency has nothing to do with poverty or riches, but arises from a basic psychological need that knows no economic boundaries. The underlying causes of delinquency—I cannot state it too strongly—are first, last and always emotional insecurity, lack of a loving relationship between the adolescent and his parents, and a climate of tension and strife in the home. They are not poverty, slum housing, inadequate crowded schools and other manifestations of a restricted economic situation.

Thus prevention of delinquency is within the power of all parents. Rich or poor, wherever they live and in whatever way they live, they can strive to remove the causes of delinquency long before their children are adolescents. They can prevent delinquency by their attitudes toward their children and by the atmosphere they create in their homes.

In the rehabilitation of delinquents, however, we come up against economic problems.

As some of the stories I have recounted indicate, the delinquent adolescent from a wealthy home is more apt to obtain prompt and full psychiatric help than the adolescent reared in poverty. The wealthy lad can more readily be taken away from an environment that is contributing to his delinquency, and because he is not bucking against adverse conditions his difficulty is more clear-cut and readily recognized. Psychiatric treatment given in clinics and as adjuncts to courts is good as far as it goes, but it simply does not go far enough. There are too few professional people in proportion to the many delinquents who need their services. And it is often difficult if not impossible to change the physical conditions which made it easy for the evil plant of delinquency to grow.

We must somehow help all parents understand the forces that are at work in fostering delinquency, and what they can and should do to remove these forces. We must give parents professional help, when it is needed, *before* their children become delinquents. And we must provide professional help for all adolescents who have taken the road that leads to delinquency.

CHAPTER ELEVEN

Escape into Immaturity

WHEN DOES ADOLESCENCE END and adulthood begin? In terms of years, society gives the answer by the age at which it grants its members certain rights and privileges. At twenty-one, American citizens are eligible to vote. In many states a person may marry without parental consent above the age of eighteen, and in general a person may obtain a full license to drive an automobile at eighteen, instead of the limited license issued to younger drivers. The inference from these figures is clear. Society considers a man or woman "old enough" at these ages to assume the responsibilities that go hand in hand with certain privileges.

But chronological adulthood and psychological adulthood are not identical. The first is simply a matter of years; the second is the fruit of a complex process. Psychological adulthood means that a person has passed through the successive phases of his psychological development—the phases described in this book—and has finally arrived at full development, at maturity. Sometimes a person has been caught or blocked somewhere along the road that should normally lead to the goal of maturity. As we have seen in the previous two chapters, some persons escape from their problems into neuroses and other manifestations of mental illness, others escape into delinquency. Still others escape into immaturity. They step aside, as it were, instead of continuing to the end of the journey through childhood and adolescence. They may be in their twenties or even thirties—adult in years—but they are still immature. Because of some difficulty in the earlier phases of their development, their personalities are marked by the characteristics of one of these earlier phases instead of by the characteristics of maturity.

In the closing section of this book which follows this chapter, I discuss the meaning of psychological adulthood and attempt to give a picture of a well-rounded mature person. For our purposes here, to help you understand the process of escape into immaturity, a brief sketch of a mature person will suffice. First and foremost, he has relinquished the dependency role of infancy, childhood and adolescence. He has attained emotional security, and he has established co-operative and mutually satisfying relationships of all sorts. He has already made an emotionally satisfying marriage or is ready to enter into one.

It is seldom, of course, that a person is completely mature in all facets of life. Sometimes circumstances have delayed him in attaining one of the goals of maturity. What counts is a person's general attitude toward life, his sense of responsibility, his ability to foresee and accept the consequences of whatever he does.

Illustrations of this general statement are most readily found in the area of self-support. The young man who follows his general college course with four to six years of professional training, as in the case of a physician, is still dependent economically at the age of twenty-five or twenty-six. Nevertheless, he may be considered mature, since he is working toward a definite goal and accepts the limitations as well as the advantages of his situation. Economic independence is also often delayed by the interruptions of military service. The veteran who is supported by his wife or parents while he completes his education and perhaps takes professional training is not for this reason immature. His long-range plans and definite goals, his capacity for establishing co-operative relationships, mark him as a mature adult.

With this base line, let us look at some of the adults who have not achieved maturity, who have, in effect, escaped from the realities of life by taking refuge in immaturity. There are many types.

The pleasure seeker, as I call one type, is the characteristic playboy, irresponsible, indifferent to the wishes of other people, unable to function in any give-and-take relationship. He hates work and has no sense of the value of money. Instead of earning it he gets what he needs—or tries to get it—by gambling and betting. When he wins and is "in the money" he spends it all with his cronies; when he loses, he borrows from anyone who is a sucker for his hard luck story.

Clarence, at twenty-five, is a pleasure seeker. He has drifted listlessly from job to job, and has finally given up all pretense at earning a living and establishing himself in life. He is energetic at figuring out the dope sheet on the horses, the boxing bouts, and basketball games, and a busy beaver at placing bets, but when it comes to a steady job or to preparing himself for a steady job he is inert and lazy. Still playing the child, he lives at home and lets Mama take care of him. And this she does slavishly, cooking his favorite dishes, keeping his clothes in order—in a word doing all the things that it was normal for her to do for Clarence, the child of seven, but far from normal to do for Clarence, the man in his twenties. Clarence has a great need to feel important, and his desire for the unearned buck with which to satisfy this need drives him into fantastic flights of fancy in which his parents are the victims. He *must* have $500 by tomorrow, he reports breathlessly. He owes this amount to a bookie and his life is threatened. And Clarence's parents, fearful, bewildered, half knowing he is lying, half believing his tale, dig down into their savings and give him the money. Of course, he soon loses it, and of course he soon comes back with another variation of his dramatic story. And so it goes on and on. Clarence is unable to face reality; he has escaped into perpetual immaturity.

Winthrop is also a pleasure seeker. For many years after he squeaked through college, he refused to take a job because he couldn't stand the daily grind and the regimentation. Loftily he explained that he was made for better things. Finally Winthrop's father took him into his real estate business, chiefly as a way of getting him out of the house in the morning, and started him at a salary out of all proportion to his worth. Did Winthrop try to live up to his responsibilities and learn to make himself useful? Far from it. He was soon lording it over everyone and finding fault with the way the business was run. Yet he scorned all routine tasks and was always out of the office making "business contacts," that is, having a drink with the boys. If he happened to be trapped into concerning himself with a business deal, he got someone else to direct it from the side lines and then—if the outcome was successful—took all the credit himself. Everything Winthrop did was designed to impress people in the business and on the outside with his superiority.

The perpetual college student, another type of immature man, enjoys dependency just as does the pleasure seeker, although his way of life appears on the surface to be more socially acceptable. Throughout his undergraduate course he vacillates from one "major" to another, unable to focus his interest. Still unfocused, he goes on to graduate work, supported by his parents or by a legacy, it matters not whether large or small. This type of person is not to be confused with the true scholar who has definite and mature goals. The scholar's goals are to advance the frontiers of knowledge, to dissolve however slightly the mists that obscure some area of the past or some vista into the future, to share his learning with others and to teach the young. The perpetual college student has none of these mature drives. He is selfish and self-centered, he clings to dependence and a role that makes no demands upon him. In essence, he fears competition and failure; he also fears success, for it will destroy his dependency.

If for some reason the funds that have supported him give out, the perpetual college student is likely to seek protection in a routine job with some large impersonal business organization. He is chiefly interested in obtaining a job that makes no demands upon him, a job in which he gets food, shelter, and security, and gives little in return. It is well to recall that this is the normal setup for a child. More is expected of an adult.

Another type of immature man is much concerned with his physical comforts and equates them with "freedom." Usually he gets the comforts from his mother upon whom he is wholly dependent, although he thinks that by staying at home he is achieving personal independence.

Ronald, a man of this type, was in his early thirties when he came to me for help in his marriage difficulties. Before his marriage he had lived at home with his parents, and as he described the setup it was ideal. He had a steady, not too demanding job as an accountant, and spent his evenings and holidays with his family. He fought shy of marriage. "After all," he said, "why should I have wanted to marry? I was well taken care of at home, and I could come and go as I pleased." Ronald was unaware, as he told me his story, that he had been utterly dependent and that the home situation had seemed ideal to him because it was a child's protected life. When he was thirty his parents died within a few months of each other. Alone and lost, missing his mother's care, his father's attention, he married and was amazed and hurt that he did not find in his new situation a replica of the old one. Naturally, his wife did not play the mother's role to his satisfaction, and so the marriage began to founder. This story, I am glad to say, had a happy ending. Ronald eventually understood the forces that had shaped his life and slowly learned to face the realities of adulthood.

The perfectionist and the man who needs constant reassurance are both immature. Their salient personality traits are hangovers from childhood. Both these types run into difficulties on the job. To the perfectionist, the office system—no matter where he works—is inefficient; his superiors are dumb and his colleagues even dumber. He is at odds with everyone, feeling superior and taking no pains to hide his feelings. Small wonder that he finds himself losing one job after another. The man who is always seeking reassurance is also in trouble on the job. He wants approval and to get it he is a sucker for overtime work, for taking on other people's tasks and letting himself get pushed around. As a result, he is tense, anxious, worried, and too tired at the close of work to have any kind of satisfactory personal life. Despite all his efforts each job finally becomes too much for him, and he, too, flits from one job to another without giving—or getting—satisfaction. The old saying about being able to work with, over or under another person is applicable here. A person who can function in this way is mature. He can take responsibility, he can carry out orders, he can be part of a team. The immature person cannot.

Immaturity in a man shows up not only in his work but also—and more importantly—in his choice of a wife and in the kind of marriage he makes. Thinking only of himself and unwilling to accept the responsibilities of supporting a family, the immature man often seeks economic security through marriage to a girl of means, regardless of his feelings. The Horatio Alger stories so popular a generation ago were all concerned with the poor boy who marries the boss's daughter. It was the success element in those stories that made them into the great American saga. No one, to my knowledge, pointed out that by taking this road to success the manly "hero" was only covering up his immaturity.

Far from solving his problems by marrying for wealth, the immature man only creates greater difficulties for himself. In one way or another he and his wife are unable to achieve a wholesome, satisfactory marriage. John-who-marries-a-rich-girl may go into his father-in-law's business instead of striking out for himself as a more independent person would do. Then he may bolster himself by feeling very important, having an exaggerated idea of his worth, and concluding that he is being unfairly treated in regard to salary and authority. He may take the opposite tack and be overwhelmed by a sense of his own inadequacy, and by fear that the boss—his wife's father—will catch him making mistakes. Sometimes he takes refuge in illness, and develops neurotic disabilities that give him a good excuse to stay away from work. His illness also forces his wife to take care of him and makes him the object of sympathy from family and friends. Sometimes the poor fellow covers up his feeling of inferiority by playing the superior he-man role at home. He goes into tirades at the least sign of household carelessness, complains that he could have married "better"—meaning a richer girl—and that his life is ruined. A further variation of the situation is for the man to identify himself with his rich father-in-law and to make his wife a dependent little girl. He is incapable of treating her as an equal; she is shoved down into playing the child, who must obey, and who is scolded or praised according to how she carries out her husband's wishes.

I have thus far discussed various types of immature men. What about immature women? Somehow, a woman's need to give to others, her innate maternal drive seems to save her from many of the manifestations of immaturity. It is chiefly in her personal relationships that immaturity shows itself. Married or unmarried she may be narcissistic—wanting always to be the center of attraction, interested only in herself. She may be a perfectionist—nagging constantly in a futile effort to have everything "just so," and giving no heed to whether or not this makes for happiness. She may be stingy—holding the purse strings, unable to spend for her own or others' pleasure even when there is no financial stringency. She may be a Calamity Jane, pessimistic, fearsome, always expecting that things will go wrong.

Each one of these traits, you will recall, is characteristic of a phase of infancy or childhood. The immature young woman has not sloughed them off although she has become an adult in years.

Immaturity in a woman shows up most clearly and perhaps most tragically in three areas—her inability to choose a mate or her unsuitable choice, the homemaking sphere and the marriage relationship. I use the phrase "inability to choose a mate," despite the fact that I am well aware of the numerical discrepancy in many communities between the number of so-called available men and available women. To explore this sociological situation would take us far afield. For our purposes, we must focus on why one woman marries and another does not, why some women, widowed or divorced, marry a second time while others do not marry even once. It is too simple to dismiss the problem by saying that there are not enough men. A girl is often prevented from choosing a mate by preoccupation with her image of the ideal husband—who of course does not exist. Perhaps she feels so superior that no one is good enough for her, or perhaps she is the perpetual virgin, untouchable and withdrawing from even the idea of marital relations. All these traits are hangovers from early phases of development, and such hangovers are, as I have tried to make clear, signs of immaturity.

I discussed above the man who marries a wealthy girl, and his motives for doing so. A girl may also marry for money, but her motives are somewhat different. Although she may want wealth and economic security, her basic drive is to be loved, and money is only a means to that end—however fallacious the idea is—not an end in itself. A girl who marries an unloved "rich man" is perhaps acting out early phantasies of being a princess rescued from a life of poverty; she is perhaps trying to provide herself with the protecting father she did not have as a child.

The age relationship of marriage partners also gives us some clue to whether one or the other is immature. In a wholesome marriage, husband and wife are generally about the same age—give or take a year or two—or at most about five years apart in age. When the difference is very great, we may suspect that the younger partner identifies the older one with his or her parent of the opposite sex.

Percy in his young twenties married a woman of forty, "old enough to be his mother," as the saying goes. He expected his wife to take up where his mother left off, to treat him as a child, to give him guidance, advice and unstinting support. Naturally, he called her "Mama." As it happened, his wife was willing to play the mother role in which Percy cast her, and so, on the surface, all went well with the marriage. But this son-mother relationship lacked the elements essential in a good marriage. Wanting always to be a small boy with a mother at hand, Percy was immature.

Similarly, a girl who marries a much older man is generally trying to provide herself with a father rather than a mate. She is too immature—or, let us say, she is not yet mature enough— for the partnership of marriage. Still a child, psychologically speaking, she wants to be protected and cared for by a "father."

The phrase "not yet mature enough" is the key to what often happens in marriages with extreme age differences. The younger person may finally "grow up," and then the marriage that seemed so right and indeed *was* right for an immature person is no longer satisfactory. The inevitable limitations of age in the older partner add to the difficulties. The mother-wife and the father-husband in their sixties no longer have the sexual drive, the energy and resilience of their younger spouses. Instead of the comfort and satisfaction that was found in the marriage at the beginning, there is unhappiness and disappointment, probably arguments, recriminations and open warfare. Often the couple does not know why things have changed. They do not realize that the marriage, based on the younger partner's immaturity and the older partner's acquiescence to this immaturity, no longer serves. Such marriages often end in divorce, and the younger person, now mature, marries a contemporary.

The same kind of difficulties can arise even when husband and wife are approximately the same age. Larry is just a year older than Joan. When the wedding bells rang, everything pointed toward a successful marriage. But as soon as the couple set up housekeeping, trouble reared its ugly head. Larry expected Joan to run the house just the way his mother did, to cook the things he liked, whether or not she liked them, to manage without any outside help even though they could well afford a weekly cleaning woman. He brushed off all of Joan's suggestions and demands for the household appliances modern young women take for granted—a washing machine, a pressure cooker, a vacuum cleaner, an electric mixer. His mother never had these things, he said. His mother did all her own housework, and made clothes, put up jam and pickles, and stoked a coal range besides. She was busy from morning till night, he said fatuously, and she never complained. Joan may have thought to herself, The poor thing, how dumb can one be. She may have said, "Because your mother made a slave of herself, is no reason why you should expect me to do the same." One word led to another, and Larry and Joan were soon launched on a good knock-down-and-drag-out fight. What they were really fighting about, of course, had nothing to do with cleaning and cooking. They were in trouble because Larry in his immaturity could only play the role of a small boy and he wanted his wife to play the role of his mother. And Joan resented being forced to play that role; she resented the fact that she had unwittingly taken on a child when she thought she was to have a mate.

Animosity toward in-laws is another sign of immaturity. The prevalence of mother-in-law jokes indicates that this kind of maladjustment is widespread. The man who fights with his mother-in-law, who enjoys telling jokes at her expense, is really hostile toward his own mother as was natural at an early phase of his development. He is unconscious of this hostility and has transferred it to his wife's mother; he has also probably transferred some of it to his wife. Similarly, the wife who "cannot get along" with her mother-in-law is not really at odds with her because she shines the pots and does the mending, thus indirectly criticizing her daughter-in-law's housekeeping. She is really spilling over onto her husband's mother the hostility she felt toward her own mother but did not express and very likely did not realize she had.

The situations I have described are examples of the many ways in which immaturity of either the man or the woman prevents them from achieving a good marriage relationship. It would be impossible to discuss all of them. We must, however, consider one further manifestation—the inability to participate in satisfying sexual intercourse. The man and woman who have successfully passed through the psychological stages of development—who are mature—are capable of good sexual functioning. Their sexual drives are part of their love relationship, an outgrowth of their love. When sex feelings and love are merged, the sexual act is an experience of satisfaction and ecstasy. It is followed, for both the man and the woman, by feelings of serenity, optimism, tenderness and fondness for the partner—and later by the wish to sleep.

A man may be considered impotent and a woman frigid if they are unable to participate in intercourse in this way. If, in either case, there is no evidence of physical impairment, the cause must be sought in the psychological sphere. I use the term impotence in its broad functional sense as meaning: the inability to become sexually stimulated, to obtain and maintain an erection, to go on to the ejaculation of the seminal fluid in a way that results in a feeling of well-being (an orgasm) for the female as well as for the male. Inability to achieve *any one* of these phases of intercourse may be considered impotence. Frigidity denotes partial or total inability of the woman to obtain an orgasm. The term must be thus qualified, since some women are capable of having an occasional orgasm, others rarely have one, and still others never have one. In a small number of cases, the difficulty is caused by some ovarian or endocrine disturbance. In the great majority, however, it is caused by emotional immaturity. Moreover, in the comparatively few instances where there is an organic difficulty, there is also generally an emotional difficulty which persists even after the organic disturbance has been corrected.

We can best understand the manifestations of impotence in the male by considering them with reference to the developmental phase in which his immaturity is fixated.

Bearing in mind the characteristics of the oral phase, here are a few examples of what happens when a man is fixated at this phase. The narcissist, who has a tremendous amount of self-love, is interested during intercourse only in his own pleasure and is completely indifferent about how his wife feels. He may indulge frequently, not on the basis of love, but merely to prove how wonderful he is. The omnipotent man likewise thinks only of himself, and his chief interest in intercourse is to prove to himself that he is sexually capable. As a result he gets only an animalistic satisfaction entirely devoid of any elements of love. The exhibitionist and the glutton are also poor sexual partners. The exhibitionist is in love with his own body and he has no concern for anyone else, and the glutton is so preoccupied with his love for food that he has no interest in or energy for the sexual function. The deprived, anxious man is certain that he will function poorly, and so he wants to complete the sex act as speedily as possible. Because of his anxiety, he can get no pleasure from intercourse and can give none to his wife.

Fixation at the anal phase may also make a man impotent. A person fixated at this phase may be a hypochondriac or a perfectionist, he may be compulsive, obstinate or sadistic. These characteristics show up in his sexual relations.

The hypochondriac, preoccupied with his bodily ills, fears that intercourse will drain away his strength. He is likely to abstain entirely or to participate as infrequently as possible. In the latter case he goes through the sex act as quickly as possible, getting no pleasure from it and giving none. The overly precise and overly efficient man (the perfectionist) cannot be spontaneous in his sex life, he cannot "waste" anything. So he usually makes a definite appointment with his wife for intercourse at a specified time several days ahead. When the time comes, he is in a hurry—to his mind, efficient— and like the hypochondriac he gets and gives no pleasure. The obstinate man shows his impotence in precisely the opposite way. Determined not to give up his semen in intercourse, he prolongs the sexual act and hence thinks that he is superior to other men. Actually, he is a poor sex partner because he is interested only in expressing his obstinacy and has no concern for his wife's reactions. The sadistic man fears that he may damage the woman during the sex act, because he thinks of his penis as a weapon; at the same time he wants to hurt her. Aggression and sadism are coupled with anxiety in his approach to intercourse. The compulsive man is obsessed with the idea that the sexual act is something forbidden and "dirty." Generally he has taken a vow of chastity in boyhood and he still feels that intercourse is wicked except when used to beget children. With such attitudes he is incapable of normal sexual functioning.

The man who is fixated at the phallic phase has all the feelings that were normal during boyhood but that should have been outgrown. He is convinced that his penis is small although it is normal in size. He is worried that he will be unable to function sexually, belittles his own masculinity and is crushed by a sense of his wife's superiority. The sex act is so frightening to him that he gets through with it as quickly as possible, and neither he nor his wife experiences any pleasure.

Fixation at the oedipal phase results in a man identifying all women with his mother or sister. As a result, he may abstain from intercourse entirely. When there is great idealization of the wife, the man may feel that he is not good enough for her and be unable to have sexual relations with her. When he does have intercourse within the marriage relationship he is likely to have disturbances of erection and feelings of oppression and guilt. Sometimes he is able to function only by forcing himself to think of other things—the events of the day or plans for tomorrow. In this way he unconsciously crowds out thoughts of the mother. He is capable of functioning sexually with prostitutes since he does not identify them with the mother.

Such a man has probably during early childhood seen his parents in the sex act while in a crib in their bedroom. The effects of this "witnessing of the primal scene," as it is technically called, is disastrous. Actually, he would prefer to watch the sex act than participate, although he may not realize that this is the case. Parents are too prone to assume that the young child in their bedroom is asleep and unaware of what is going on. The child, however, often sees the sex act. It is of course incomprehensive and frightening, and the effect on him is generally far-reaching and tragic. I want to say with all the emphasis I can bring to bear on this topic that children, however young they are, should not share the parental bedroom and should never see their parents having intercourse.

The man who is fixated at early adolescence, the homosexual phase, tends to take a passive role during intercourse. He has much anxiety and usually has a quick orgasm, as if to get through the sex act as speedily as possible. On the following day he is generally hostile toward his wife because, unconsciously, he resents the fact that she has made him take the male role.

There is also the "ardent lover." He becomes strongly infatuated with a woman he has recently met. Usually, he discovers that she is already married, has been married or is at present attached to some other man. He is profuse in his love for her. He showers her with attention, gifts, continuous phone calls, and convinces her of his fervent love. He is unrelenting in his sincere attention to win her. She is finally so completely carried away by his ardor and show of affection that she submits to the sex act. He is able to function, but with anxiety, excitement and a quick termination. The next day, his love for her seems to have cooled. He admits to himself he was disappointed. After all, she did not coincide with his "ideal image" of woman. Actually he is not interested in this woman. Unconsciously he is interested in the man to whom she is attached, and he is eager to have sexual contact with him as though to satisfy a homosexual need. He can no longer return to this woman, and now puts his efforts on wooing and winning another one. Such is the psychology of the Don Juan, fixated at the homosexual phase.

The incestuous guilt feelings that come from fixation at the phase of middle adolescence may lead a man into tremendous sexual curiosity about other people instead of normal sexual functioning. Often this curiosity is shifted, in a socially acceptable way, to rare possessions and a passion for collecting. The insatiable collector speaks of his possessions as a lover would speak of a woman, and to him an object is "most beautiful" if it is so rare that no one else could possess anything like it. Such attitudes suggest the desire to possess the unattainable mother—the most beautiful and desirable woman to the boy in middle adolescence.

Frigidity in women—the counterpart of male impotence—is likewise a manifestation of immaturity. What form it takes depends on the phase of development at which a woman is fixated.

The woman who is a narcissist is passive during intercourse. She craves love, as a baby does, but is incapable of giving love. During the sex act she is only interested in determining how much her husband loves her and has no concern for achieving mutual pleasure. Another type of woman shows her oral fixation by constant chatter during intercourse and she is very likely to use this opportunity to tell her husband about something she has seen and would dearly love to have. She eats candy or sucks a sourball and often smokes a cigarette. Like a baby, she makes known her wants and satisfies them through her mouth. And then there is the self-sufficient woman who actually does not need a man. She participates regularly and willingly in intercourse, but without an orgasm, and finds some pretext to send her husband out of the room as soon as the sex act is over. While he is gone and without his knowing it, she masturbates. Her self-sufficiency is so great that she rejects normal sexual functioning.

The characteristics of pessimism and fear that characterize the late oral phase are shown in the woman who dreads intercourse. She approaches her first sex experience with anxiety, and sex intercourse remains for her a nightmare, dreaded and feared. The same forces are at work in the woman who is afraid of pregnancy. Even when contraceptives are used, she is sure that they will fail, and she lives in a continuous state of anxiety that prevents good sexual functioning.

As a result of fixation at the anal phase, some women can participate in the sex act only if they think of something "dirty." A constant exchange of obscene words heightens their excitation and makes orgasm possible. Another type of woman very tactfully and politely finds reasons for postponing intercourse—it is late, she is tired, tomorrow night would be better, and so on. She finally gives in, but with bad grace, urging her husband to "hurry up" so she can get some sleep. She does not experience the slightest pleasure in intercourse; actually she rejects it.

During the phallic phase a girl feels bewildered and inadequate because she has no penis, and she sometimes tried to hide this lack from herself and others by not exposing her body. The prudish woman is fixated at this phase. She will never undress before her husband and she makes sure that the bedroom is in complete darkness before she will have intercourse. She wants no fondling and demands that there be no noise and no talking for fear (she says) that the children or the neighbors may hear something. Even in a hotel room, she is afraid that the unknown "people in the next room" may hear what is going on.

The counterpart of the man who is fixated at the homo-sexual early adolescent phase is the woman who plays the masculine role in all her daytime activities. But during inter-course she must be a woman, despite her psychological inclina-tions. Since she cannot accept her own femininity, she detests her husband for having forced her into the female role, and on the day following intercourse she invariably shows her irrita-tion by nagging and faultfinding.

In middle adolescence, you will recall, a girl is in love with her father and sees her mother as a rival for his attention and love. In her desire to take her mother's place, she identi-fies with her. There is the dutiful wife who thinks she must "submit" to her husband and do whatever he wants her to do, in order to please him. She has no concept of the sex act as something in which husband and wife share a rewarding expe-rience. Although she acquiesces whenever her husband wants intercourse, she actually rejects both her husband and the sex act itself. The motherly type of woman expresses her identifi-cation with her own mother more openly. She is usually the aggressor in intercourse, but in a sweet, genteel and encourag-ing way. During the sex act she keeps up a constant murmur of praise, saying "That's a good boy. Oh, how wonderful you are," stroking and soothing her husband and commending him. When intercourse is over, she emphasizes how happy she is that he has enjoyed it, inferring that her only concern is his pleasure. She is content to play the self-effacing role and has no concept of the mutuality of the sex experience.

What may be termed the intellectual type of woman par-ticipates in the sex act because she reasons that nature intended man and woman to have intercourse; there is no emotional involvement. To some women of this type the sex act is an all-night orgy. Everything goes. Spirits are high and they have no prohibitions and nothing to suppress. The entire thing is an affair of laughter and fun. They diversify their ways of carrying out the sex act and they also diversify their partners on the basis that "variety is the spice of life." Since the concept of love is entirely lacking, such antics, which may even go as far as switching partners, seems to them entirely natural.

The prostitute type of woman also has no concept of the love element in intercourse. She participates with her husband whenever he wishes, but at a price. She sells her body just as the prostitute does. The woman who goes from one man to another and is never satisfied is called nymphomaniac. One type experiences a tremendous amount of excitement during intercourse but is unable to reach orgasm. So she flits from man to man in the hope that she will find a partner who can help her have a complete sexual experience. The second type is able to arrive at orgasm and yet never has enough sex to satisfy her. She indulges so frequently that the man is drained and worn out sexually; but she is still eager for further intercourse. So she finds another partner and starts all over again. Such a woman's deep inner psychology is that she wants to take away every man's masculinity. By making men weaklings she proves her superiority to all men. And then there is the woman who is completely numb physically and has no erotic feeling during the entire sexual act. Her disgust mounts and when the act is over she must dash to the bathroom and vomit. She is unable to sleep and has a severe headache on the following day.

Immaturity manifests itself in still another aspect of married life—the attitude of husband and wife toward the coming of their first child. Let us assume that the couple want a child and that the pregnancy was planned. When husband and wife are mature and have developed a wholesome marriage relationship, there is joyful anticipation of the "blessed event," and plans are made both for the pregnancy and for the care of the baby. What happens when the man or woman are immature?

The man thinks of the unborn child as an interloper. He remembers his own childhood when he was unable to get his mother's exclusive love because she also loved his father. He recalls how he hated her for failing to give him all the attention he wanted. News of his own child's coming revives the mingled emotions of love and hate that he had known in childhood.

All the difficulties between husband and wife at this time are rooted in this revival of conflicting emotions. A man may start by finding fault with his wife about small unimportant things. Soon he is openly hostile to her and loses control of his pent-up emotions. He slaps her, pushes her and even beats her. He may take to drink and abuse her as though getting some sort of satisfaction at being himself the baby—in this case the naughty baby. Sometimes news of his wife's pregnancy drives a man into extramarital relationships although he has previously been faithful to his wife. He justifies his actions by convincing himself that he needs to release his sexual tensions during the months when he cannot have sexual relations with his wife. Actually he fears the loss of his wife's love and turns to other women in the hope that he can get from them what he thinks he is losing in his marriage. He is also driven by a vague desire to "get even" with his wife. Occasionally an immature man reacts to his wife's pregnancy by anxiety, pessimism and depression, in an unconscious effort to force her to focus her attention on him instead of on the child. The neurotic manifestations of his conflicts and confusions may be so severe that he must have psychiatric care.

The wholesome mature woman follows her doctor's "do's and don'ts" of pregnancy, goes through this period with little or no discomfort, and looks forward with joy to the birth of her child. The immature woman begins to vomit. She does not realize that her vomiting is a psychological rejection of the pregnancy—an unconscious attempt to starve the foetus. Some women actually induce the vomiting because they cannot bear to be misshapen by pregnancy or because they have an all-pervading fear of dying during labor—they would rather destroy the baby than be themselves destroyed. Sometimes the immature pregnant woman willfully disobeys the rules of good health by excessive exercise, late hours and drinking. She may avoid all social contacts, feeling that people will be "disgusted" at how she looks. She may have crying spells and be depressed —actually she is suffering from the fear that her husband and relatives will show more affection for the baby than for her. The masculine type of woman, who has denied her femaleness but must now in motherhood accept this role, is likely to be openly hostile to her husband. Ostensibly the basis of her hostility is that he is responsible for her pains, discomforts and misshapen body; actually the basis is that he has made her a female.

Immaturity also shows itself in the parents' attitudes toward their children during infancy, childhood and adolescence. These attitudes have already been discussed in Chapter VII, "Adjustment to Parents, Brothers and Sisters."

The reader may perhaps feel that the matters discussed in this chapter, the stories of maladjusted people and warped lives, are pessimistic and disturbing. Happily, it is possible to end in a more hopeful key. Experience shows that for the most part men and women do not stay immature throughout their lives. They tend to resolve many of their conflicts by their mid-thirties. They accept their limitations and adjust to reality, and thus they are able to function in a more normal, wholesome way. Since this is what usually happens, escape into immaturity is not final and irrevocable. Men and women step aside somewhere along the road to adulthood, but they can return and complete the journey. Development has not been stopped, it has only been delayed. Immature people—sometimes by their own efforts and sometimes with outside help—can finally become mature.

On to Maturity

IN PART I OF THIS BOOK we have followed the boy and girl who
develop normally—Jimmie and Sally—on their journey through
infancy, childhood and adolescence, and have left them at the
threshold of psychological adulthood. In describing their
journey, I have tried to give you some understanding of the
forces that shaped their personalities. We have also considered,
in Part II, how circumstances—some that can be avoided or
rectified, and some that are beyond control—may thwart normal development and impede the journey from infancy to
adulthood. Here, too, I have tried to give you some understanding of the forces at work; I have explained how some adolescents stray or "escape" into dead-end roads, and how they
can generally retrace their steps and reach the goal of maturity.

Fundamentally, the mature person utilizes the many and
varied attributes of all the phases of his development for constructive purposes. He is no longer emotionally dependent, as
he was in infancy, childhood and adolescence. He is emotionally secure. He has long-range plans and definite goals and is
able to establish co-operative and mutually satisfying relationships of all sorts. He is capable of adjustment—to the affairs of
day-by-day living, to his own capacities, to economic and
physical circumstances, and to the customs and regulations of
society. Adjustment, in this sense, does not mean a slavish and
static acceptance of "things as they are" or a resigned feeling
that "all is for the best in the best of all possible worlds." On
the contrary, it means continuing growth based on a realistic

understanding of oneself and society. With that understanding, a person will have self-confidence and at the same time the self-discipline that enables him constantly to improve himself. He will function well at work and at play, he will be able to make and keep friends. He will have a social point of view and the courage to do something about conditions that he thinks should be changed. Finally, he will be able to plan for the future, establish a home, and repeat the life cycle through children.

What do these generalities mean when they are applied to actual people? Let us try to answer the question by rejoining Jimmie and Sally, who made the journey from infancy through adolescence successfully. We know what they were like as adolescents and why they behaved the way they did. What are they like now, on their way to maturity?

Jimmie—now called Jim—can get himself up in the morning at whatever time is required. He bathes, shaves, dresses without too great a struggle. He is well-groomed, and his clothes are appropriate for whatever he is going to do. If he is to spend the working day in a business office, his suit is pressed, his shirt is clean and his shoes are shined. He has exercised some choice and taste in the color combination and style of his clothes. If he is headed for a factory job or a day's fishing, he dresses differently, it goes without saying. In any case, just before leaving home, he takes one long look in the mirror and is pleased with what he sees.

Sally, too, tries to look her best, and she does not begrudge the time and money spent on being well groomed and appropriately dressed. She is not a slave to the whims of fashion, but within reason she keeps in step, picking and choosing what is most becoming. If "they" are wearing large hats and sheaths, she does not, simply from perversity, insist on billowy skirts and a Juliet cap. She pays close attention to how her dress, shoes, stockings and accessories fit together and strives for a pleasing ensemble. Sally wears a low-cut evening blouse to a dinner party but not to the office for a day at work; she wears high-heeled slippers for a dance, comfortable loafers for a hike in the country, and so on. However rushed she is, she takes time for lipstick and powder, and she experiments expertly with how best to "make up her face." Before starting out to work or play she has a final look at herself. Undoubtedly she smiles at the well-turned-out girl in the looking glass.

Both Jim and Sally enjoy good food. They have their preferences, of course, as all of us have, but they do not waste time and energy in too much talk or thought about how they can't stand spinach and why they won't eat liver. Sally is interested in improving her cooking skill and is always ready to try out new dishes, and Jim also knows his way about in the kitchen. They are not, however, preoccupied with food. A special party meal is enjoyed and then forgotten, not recalled and talked about for days and weeks after the event.

You will realize, I am sure, that I have been describing ways in which the narcissism and orality of infancy are used constructively in maturity. Our young people also enjoy other oral pleasures. Like all of us, they sing under the shower, fleetingly feeling that they have wonderful voices. They enjoy group singing, at banquets or at home, and especially around a campfire. Smoking is also a pleasure, the more so if they can blow smoke rings. They have enough poise to express their thoughts in a group without feeling self-conscious. They enjoy the feeling that people are listening to them, but they are more concerned with getting their ideas across than with making an impression.

The young child's desire to be loved carries over into maturity in the form of cordiality and friendliness toward others. Jim and Sally are able to express their affection, they are spontaneously considerate of others, gracious and kindly. The phrase "a warm, outgoing person" has much meaning. Such a person has retained from childhood the natural desire to be loved, but expresses it in a reciprocal way. He has a genuine feeling of belonging in whatever social setting he finds himself. He need not struggle for eminence, because he feels on an equal footing with those around him.

Jim and Sally have lost the infant's fear of being abandoned, and their sense of belonging is so firm that they do not mind being alone physically. If Sally is living alone and trying to "like it," she has no panicky feeling that she must have a date every evening or that a solitary meal is a catastrophe to be avoided at all costs. Jim, too, is not completely dependent upon his companions. He and Sally can live with themselves as well as with other people; they have inner resources that make them, at times, welcome solitude. They do not find it necessary to escape from themselves through being constantly on the go.

Both of our young people are on fairly even keel emotionally. They have outgrown the mood fluctuations of childhood and adolescence, and they do not swing for no discernible cause from high elation to deep depression. In times of great joy or grief, they react appropriately, of course, but for the long run, they maintain a consistent and even mood.

Orderliness and cleanliness, inculcated in childhood, become in maturity a means to an end, not an end in themselves. If Sally keeps house, she does a good job and keeps things clean and neat. She knows, however, that a home is made to live in, and is not an exhibition house in which everything must be just so. The disarray of the living room at the end of an evening—the overflowing ash trays, the empty beer glasses, the squashed-down sofa cushions—do not disturb her. They

mean to her that people have been enjoying themselves, not
that the place is "a mess." Sally keeps her bureau drawers
straight, but if she disarranges them while dressing hurriedly for
an important date she is not too upset. She normally makes
her bed before going to work, but if she oversleeps once in a
while and must dash out and leave it unmade the omission is
not an unpardonable sin that haunts her throughout the day.
Jim, too, is orderly and neat, but he uses these attributes as
tools. He is not so obsessed with being clean that he shudders
at getting his hands smeared with grease while fixing his car,
or so meticulous about neatness that he cannot tolerate a
cluttered desk—when clutter is necessary for the work at hand.

In similar fashion, the routines and disciplines established
in childhood carry over into maturity and make it possible
to function efficiently but without rigidity. Jim gets to work
at a definite time if this is required, without sputtering about
regimentation, but if for some reason he is thrown off schedule
at starting or quitting time he accepts this break in his routine
with flexibility. In a word, he can catch the 8:19 every morning without undue agony, but if he misses it because the car
won't start or the water heater went haywire, he is adjustable
enough to take it in stride. If Sally is to meet a friend for lunch
at one o'clock, she won't have hysterics if her friend is five
minutes late; on the other hand she won't manage her affairs so
ineptly that she herself invariably arrives an hour late, panting
and full of poor excuses.

More important than these adjustments to the affairs of
everyday life is the capacity to accept responsibility and to
carry through whatever task is undertaken, the ability to enjoy
one's work, and the willingness to share one's self and one's
possessions with others. The mature person has these attributes.
He also has a realistic approach to physical health and illness.

Without preoccupation or faddism, he follows the precepts of good hygiene in regard to sleep, food and exercise, and if he is ill he seeks competent medical advice and follows it.

Jim and Sally, as they approach maturity, are learning to assess their own capacities realistically. They understand their own worth without false modesty and recognize their own limitations. If Jim has a flair for selling, let us say, he develops it and tries to be a better and better salesman. He does not daydream about being a research chemist, or envy his friend who is a brilliant short story writer. The same holds true if Jim is the chemist and his friend is the salesman, of course. He may, however, be a square peg in a round hole and be doing work for which he is not suited. Instead of bemoaning his lot, he makes long-range plans for training himself in another field, even though the change may be difficult and require great sacrifice of effort and time. Whatever he is doing, Jim has confidence in himself. He is neither arrogant nor unduly timid. He knows that anyone can make mistakes in new situations, and that it is better to make them and learn from experience than to run away or be frozen into inaction by conflict and anxiety.

What I have said about Jim holds true for Sally, too. She is ambitious in the best sense of the term. She has realistic goals and is willing to work to attain them—and she does not daydream about being an opera singer, for example, if she has no voice. Whatever she is called upon to do—whether an outside job or running a household—she tries to do it as skillfully as possible and she also tries constantly to improve herself.

When a little child recounts something that has happened, he acts out what every one said, he seems impelled to be little Johnnie, the teacher, the policeman, the dog. The immature person, like the child, has a chameleonlike quality. In the company of longshoremen at the corner saloon he tries to talk tough; with a group of college professors, he tries to talk like a recent graduate of Oxford. He agrees, he quotes authority, and he never speaks his own mind. He fools no one, of course. It is obvious that he is acting, and that he is not a "genuine article." He behaves in this way because he is uncertain of himself. Jim and Sally have enough self-confidence to be themselves in any situation, to have their own way of talking, and, on a deeper level, to accept their own personalities. This means that they do their own thinking, form their own opinions and are willing to express them. Jim does not run with the hares and hunt with the hounds on questions of public importance. He informs himself, comes to conclusions, and is willing to express them. In doing so, he is not swayed by a sense of rivalry with other people, or by a need to get the better of them and make a play for special attention. He can accept people of all kinds and trust them.

The mature person extends the love he once had for his family to embrace an ever wider circle. Our ideal—lived up to by the few truly great and mature figures of history—is to love all humanity and feel that the entire world is one's home. None of us, I venture to say, will attain this ideal—but we can strive for it.

The curiosity of childhood, the eagerness to learn, and the feeling that the world is full of interesting and exciting things is carried over into maturity. Jim and Sally do not feel that their days of studying and learning are over because they have finished their formal schooling. They will continue to learn, to acquire new skills, to enlarge their horizons. They will never take refuge, later in life, in the cliché about old dogs that cannot be taught new tricks. Their lives will be enriched in many ways because they are receptive to new ideas and new activities.

The young people are no longer ambivalent, as they were in adolescence. They have transformed this quality into the capacity to evaluate the pros and cons of whatever situation arises, to assess it objectively, and to form conclusions on the basis of facts—not phantasy. Jim can get along with other men, without a feeling of rivalry; Sally makes women friends, and does not see in every girl someone who may snatch her young man away. Jim can think of women as people, as well as women, and can associate with them as fellow human beings. With this mature attitude, he feels at ease if he finds himself in a gathering where he is the only man; he does not take refuge in wise-cracks about crashing into a hen party. For the time being he is with people, not women. Sally has comparable attitudes about men.

The adolescent's preoccupation with his physical self, his worry about being too tall or too short, and about not being good-looking, largely disappears as our young people progress toward maturity. The mature person accepts himself; because he can assess himself realistically, he is not preoccupied with his physical attributes. If Jim has bushy red hair, he wastes no time daydreaming about how much more attractive he would be with straight blond hair that would stay neatly parted. If Sally has a snub nose, she doesn't worry about it and spend endless hours thinking of how wonderful it would be to have a straight-from-the-forehead Grecian nose. An inner accept-ance of themselves keeps Jim and Sally from focusing on unim-portant physical attributes, and their sense of realism keeps them from phantasy about what cannot be changed.

I have already spoken about the mature person's continu-ing desire to learn and improve himself. Jim and Sally seek knowledge and skills that will help them advance in their chosen occupations, and serve as steppingstones to the goal of self-support. They do not have an attitude of know-it-all, or of boredom about intellectual matters. On the contrary, their interests range far and wide and embrace not only areas that are of practical use to them but also those that will give them interesting occupations for their leisure time.

As our young people approach maturity they recognize that no one is independent, but that all people are interdependent. With this approach, they can accept constructive criticism on the job and in their social life. They develop friendships that are mutually satisfying, that offer for both parties the opportunity to express themselves openly with an assurance of being understood. The celebrity chaser, the man who tries to make friends with "important" people so that he can be a name-dropper, is immature. He is trying to bolster himself, to cover up his sense of insecurity.

The mature person concerns himself with politics and government. He exercises his right to vote and uses it intelligently. He informs himself on important issues, takes an active part in supporting measures that seem to him necessary for the public welfare. He accepts the decisions of the majority with good grace, but he does not relinquish the right to try to change, by lawful means, any decision which seems to him to be unwise. In his own community, the mature person is active in bettering conditions that affect his neighbors as well as himself. He does his share of the grueling and time-consuming work of serving on boards and committees, arranging meetings, and the like. He is concerned with housing, schools, recreation services for children, hospitals—in a word, everything that will help not only himself but others to have a more satisfying life.

Let us, now, try to sum up the meaning of maturity, pinpoint the motivation of the mature person. He learns to live by the golden rule. He is honest in his dealings with other people, he is kindly disposed toward all mankind. He makes no distinction in his feelings about people because of their race, creed or color. To him, all people are fellow members of the human family. He is a religious person. When he is called upon to act as a leader in any group effort, he can do so; and when someone else is the leader, he accepts the role of follower. With such attitudes, he can function in a group, large or small, and can make a constructive contribution to society.

In the personal sphere, the mature man and woman can establish an emotionally satisfying marriage. I have touched upon various aspects of marriage throughout this book and need not enlarge upon them here. Husband and wife, when both are mature, have mutual respect for one another, their two personalities are integrated, and, as a couple, they are a wholesome unit. And they have the desire for children.

Mature people develop a mode of living in keeping with their earning capacities. They do not live beyond their means. They spend without being profligate and save without hoarding. They take time out for fun—and they can relax and be lazy without feeling uneasy and guilty. They develop an avocation that gives them a feeling of creating something—it matters not whether it is painting pictures, making tables in the cellar workshop, hooking rugs, growing African violets, or reading. Few of us are artists in the strict sense of the word. Yet all of us want and need to feel creative. Our leisure time should give us this pleasure.

Jim and Sally are on their way toward maturity, and they will, I hope, continue to become more mature throughout their lives. Maturity is not a fixed state. It is a process of continuous growth. Each of us can strive for ever more maturity. It is well worth the effort, for as we grow in maturity, so do we achieve —for ourselves and for others—ever more satisfaction and happiness.